Waiting for Jeffrey

Waiting for Jeffrey

Alan Coren

ROBSON BOOKS

First published in Great Britain in 2002 by Robson Books Ltd, 64 Brewery Road, London N7 9NT

A member of **Chrysalis** Books plc

British Library Cataloguing in Publication Data
A catalogue record for this title is available from the British Library

ISBN 1 86105 595 1

Typeset by FiSH Books, London
Printed and bound in Great Britain by
Creative Print & Design (Wales), Ebbw Vale

For
No. FF 8282

Contents

Introduction

"He's NOT Jesus —— he's a very naughty boy!"
Life of Brian

Even as I write, he is writing too. I know this, because he never stops writing. And I know that, because word has come to me —— inside a cake, since you ask —— that he has already completed, in hardly more than a year, three fat books. You will say, impossible, this is just one more whopper, even his cakes are incapable of stopping themselves from telling porkies, but you are wrong. You really must learn to trust people, you know.

Sometimes, in the stilly watches of the night, when I am hunched over a keyboard desperately struggling to decide between a comma and a semicolon, I raise my head, and cock an ear northwards from my London attic, and seem to hear him, umpteen miles away, scribbling fit to bust. And I do mean scribbling, because he doesn't type, even if they would let him, which they won't, because the rattling of the keys might disturb his hundreds of neighbours, sleeping the sleep —— in one or two cases, at least —— of the just. So nobody rattles keys up there: except, of course, those who are paid to do it.

And yet, despite his reliance on nibs alone, he has succeeded in knocking out three blockbusters; a term the veracity of which you might, again, seek to challenge, on the grounds that he is currently in an unbustable block, but you are just being facetious, now. You know that these books, the moment they are published, will have punters queuing round the block, busting to buy them. Exactly when that moment might come, however, is uncertain: in his first day job, he was, as you might have heard, an exemplary medical orderly, and it was thus quite on the cards that the infirmary would move heaven and earth to prevent the loss of someone who, given time – which of course he has been – might prove himself a dab hand at everything from ingrowing toenails to coronary grafts. Sadly, however, because of their eagerness to keep him, the infirmary drew the line at letting him have a go at keyhole surgery, and he responded with a regretful decision, in August, to swap one kind of theatre for another. He is presently running (a job description he has made all his own) the Theatre Royal, Lincoln, on day-release: he drives himself there in his BMW, which has a built-in dictaphone capable of taking 100 words per minute.

It is thus quite possible that, come the great day when Her Majesty is allowed to hang on to him no longer, he will emerge with far more books than merely three. You again will scoff, pointing out that John Bunyan, Oscar Wilde and Adolf Hitler, while similarly banged up, could manage only three between them, but you forget that this man is not as other men are. Were he to serve his full term, though this would be not merely an inequity but also, beyond question, an iniquity, there are nevertheless countless millions of people on the outside selfish enough to dream of his not reappearing among them until he is carrying a sackful of manuscripts in each hand.

Which is the sole reason for my having cobbled this book. Because I can't tell you how very deeply I feel for those countless millions waiting around with £12.95 burning a hole in their pockets but nothing to read. All I pray is that, though it is only a small thing and mine own, it'll do until the right thing comes along.

AC

This and That

WHO is this That? A question rarely far, these days, from the lips of those whose ears are not perhaps as tuned to the ragtime beat of the schmutter business as they might be, and who thus have scant inkling of the most illustrious couturier of our time. Might he, as he seems from the look of it, be Siamese? Pham Van That, perhaps, Ding Dong That, ie, yet another of the umpteen oriental designers – Issey Miyake, Anna Sui, Yohji Yamamoto, Tommi Chow – whose skeletal gamines bestride the catwalks like rickety colossi? No, he is bigger than that. He is That.

He makes That dresses. The Duchess of York, I believe, was the first big star – some might say too big – to trundle out in one of his fabulous creations. You will, I'm sure, recall the banner headlines: "Fergie And That Dress". But there was far more Fergie than dress: as Samuel Taylor Coleridge so farsightedly put it: "Behold her bosom and half her side, a sight to dream of, not to tell!" This, however, served only to send svelter illuminati whizzing round to the great man's sweatshop, where teams of expert minimalists were doing astonishing things with paper-clips and hankies, and before long, the craning phalanxes of hacks and paparazzi were bringing us: "Liz Hurley And That Dress", "Kate Winslet And That Dress", "Patsy Kensit And That Dress", "Kelly Brook And That Dress", and, of course, "David Beckham And That Dress". The House of That was made. That was in every newspaper. That was on every channel. That was a household name. True, he was doomed to be unscrupulously ripped off, for this is ever the way in the fashion game: wannabe women who said to themselves "for two pins, I'd wear a dress like That", went and got two pins, and did. But things began to go wrong, because that is what things do. The romantic relationships of That icons began to fall apart: the centres could not hold. There was not much that That could do about it, just as there was nothing his father, who founded the company, could do when "Michael Foot And That Anorak" ruined the career of one of the finest men ever to stand at the Cenotaph looking like something his dog slept on. But as if this were not dreadful enough, things have gone really wrong now, as we all learnt on Monday, when the tabloids somehow found it in themselves to reveal that the second marriage of Carol Vorderman CBE, possibly the most remarkable woman in Britain, was at an end, purportedly because of That dress. She had worn it, but only just, at this year's Bafta awards, and had not only sparked a national debate about the state of arithmetic in Blair's Britain, but also, it is alleged, terminally upset her husband.

I cannot, of course, know whether these allegations are true, but they certainly have the ring of truth to me. Though I am still grappled to the first Mrs Coren with hoops of steel, it has often been a damn close-run thing down the long arches of the years, entirely because of

That. For I myself dress not merely in That, but also in the controversial gear of its sister company, Those. Indeed, the House of That almost put paid to our marriage before it had effectively begun. Because the firm made grey top hats, which Moss Bros hired out to impecunious grooms, and it made them so large that brides frequently failed to recognise the person whom they had just undertaken to love, honour, and obey. "Where is he?" was the first sentence uttered by the new Mrs Coren as the family arranged itself for the nuptial photograph. "He's there, next to you, under the hat," said my best man. "Well, he's not wearing That," was Mrs Coren's second sentence, and it has stood her in good stead ever since. With, of course – as you would expect after 39 blissful years – variations, according to what I have chosen and loyally continue to choose from my extensive That wardrobe. Sometimes, she is merely gently remonstrative, as in "Are you absolutely certain you're happy in That?", at other times the need comes on her to point out that Oxfam might be prepared to take Those, green corduroy may be all the rage in Burundi, but it cannot be denied that when, for some swisher gathering, I hobble down the stairs in a dinner jacket straining against the evidence of all the dinners it's been to, and a pair of glaucous shoes on which the patent ran out decades ago, she can be quite ratty, viz, "You expect me to walk in with someone wearing That, when I'm wearing This?" She always gets her clothes at This, and always looks terrific, but quite why This should have cracked it when That hasn't got the first idea, I find quite beyond comprehension.

Unless he really is Siamese, and pronounces his name Tat.

Age Unconcern

NOTHING in living memory – I cannot, of course, answer for dead memory, of which I seem to be accumulating more and more, these days – has surprised me less than the findings of the Wellbeing 2002 survey, commissioned by Boots the Chemists. Published yesterday, the survey reveals that by far the happiest generation of Britons is the one over 65. How much of a revelation is that? Of course old people are happy. Watch them. They are sliding up the banisters.

You cannot slide up the banisters if you are young. I know this, because I see an enormous amount of afternoon television, which caters predominantly for the elderly, and no matter what time of the afternoon you switch on you will see an old person sliding up the banisters on a stairlift. She – it is generally she, though not exclusively – is beaming broadly, despite the fact that she is carrying a big basketful of laundry or a big trugful of flowers. No, *because* of the fact, since she could never carry them upstairs if she didn't own a thing for sliding up the banisters on. She is also smiling because she has got a free eight-day carriage clock. You cannot see it in the film of her sliding upstairs, doubtless because she has proudly put it in her carriage, which (like her) we shall come to later, but we know that she has it because the film commentary has informed us that

4

if we buy a stairlift, we will get a free carriage clock, too.

But I cannot get either a stairlift or a carriage clock, because I am not old enough. I would feel a prat ordering it, I would feel a prat watching the men bolting it to the wall, I would feel a prat sitting in it while they tested it. I wouldn't half like one, though: my house has six floors, which, young though I am, are putting years on me. Stairwise, I am going on 90.

If the old lady sliding up the banisters – there are many different stairlifts on afternoon TV – is Dame Thora Hird, she has even more to be happy about, because she also has a bed that goes up and down. Not, of course, the way it does in youth, but electrically, with a button on a lead.

I can't tell you how much I would like that, it would be an inestimable boon when lying in bed of an afternoon watching old ladies whizzing up banisters, but I'd feel a prat. The delivery men would say: "Where do you want this then, grandpa?"

God knows what they'd say if I bought one of those baths where you get in by opening a door in the side. There are several of these on afternoon TV, used mainly by old ladies in, for some reason, swimsuits. There is one old man, mind, who comes on with a big grin, opens the door, sits down in his bath, and shuts the door again. Since he is not in a swimsuit but a bathrobe, he looks like some ancient emir getting into a state brougham, smiling smugly the whiles upon his fawning populace. Is he happy, at 75? Ecstatic.

Especially if he has a real carriage (see above) downstairs. You can get these off afternoon TV, too, if you're old; they are titchy electric karts with a nice shiny rack at the front for shopping – or simply displaying your free carriage clock to its best advantage – and you can drive them on the pavements, thus avoiding traffic jams or being dragged up before the beak for not being able to read a numberplate without nine pairs of glasses and forced to take your driving test again so that cyclists can resume banging your roof and pedestrians kicking your doors.

How I should love one of those! I'd find a Silverstone electrician to give it a bit of a tweak, belt through the Waitrose chicanes in no time and be back in my comfy self-elevating bed in a trice with my new teatime muffins sizzling in my bedside toaster – a free gift for buying an exclusively old person's annuity from the former James Herriot – as I wait happily for the great glue advert.

And I do mean great. If the Wellbeing 2002 survey had any doubts about the happiness of the aged, all they had to do was clock the smile of the woman whose teeth are glued in with the stuff that keeps the tiles on the Shuttle. I cannot buy this glue yet, however, because I still have my own teeth, and a bloody pain they are, but one day I will have a set that will make Carol Smilie look like a professional mourner, and, once they are locked in place with this terrific glue, I shall be able to open beer bottles with them, I shall be able to walk into my bath and hang by them from the shower head, I shall be able to tighten the hub-nuts on my little electric carriage, I shall be able to carry the loaded tea tray in my stairlift up to my elevating bed, despite the fact that my hands are full of laundry, flowers, and carriage clocks. I shall be so happy.

Between the Lines

READERS who have nothing better to do with their time than root around in secondhand bookshops – and how lucky they are, as we shall soon see, that they do have nothing better to do with their time – may recall that etymology is something of a hobby with me. That is how I know that the word hobby originally meant a horse; what I did not know until recently was what kind of horse it was. I now know that it is a Trojan horse: on the outside, it looks like something that wants to spot trains and collect cheese-labels, but on the inside, all it wants is a bit of how's your father.

I reach this conclusion as the result of an immense mailbag trucked round to my premises by Consignia in the wake of Monday's news that the 50,000 (*sic*) book discussion groups which have latterly mushroomed all over Britain are not always what they appear to be. Many of their half million members do not foregather in pursuit of mutual enlightenment about *Tristram Shandy* or *Finnegans Wake*; the only mutual enlightenment they seek concerns which of them is up for it. Grimmer yet, it seems that the texts are more often than not chosen for their subtextual value: pick the right plot-line and before you can say Fanny Hill, the members are at it like knives. Yet, unsettling as this may be for the authentic bibliophile, should we not have guessed? Isn't this 2002, when there is only one hobby that we are everywhere and at all times urged to pursue? Let me dip, at random, into that mailbag.

Oh, look, a letter from a Mrs Brown, of Honiton. Dear Mr Coren, she writes, I recently took up bellringing in the hope of widening my circle of acquaintances who weren't Mr Brown, and was shown the ropes (yes, you are not wrong, GSOH is one of my qualifications, plus big bust and own VW Golf) by a very nice gentleman and was well getting the hang of it, ha-ha, never passing him on the way up or down without a quip or a nudge, a meaningful relationship was well on the cards, when him and this bottle-blonde next to him suddenly give two almighty tugs and before I know it, they have shot up into the organ-loft from whence they did not re-emerge until the vicar shut up shop. What I want to ask is, would you know if hunky Rick Stein runs cookery classes and if so, does it have to be fish, due to my allergy?

Heartbreaking, you will agree, but worse than this one? Dear Mr Coren, I was coming out of the Job-Centre, no luck there, all blokes, when I saw a woman walking into the local Flat Earth Society on these really terrific legs, so I immediately joined up, and after the lecture – about Lord Lucan falling off the edge of the Bermuda Triangle – I invited her to Brighton to check on whether the horizon was curved or not. She readily agreed, but on the train down she told me that God was an onion. Am I in any danger, and if so, would it be wiser to take up community singing?

This being a tricky one to answer, I turned instead to a parcel postmarked Rhyl which I discovered came from a man who had clearly not realised quite how illegal it was to send it in the mail. He had, he explained, enrolled in a clay-modelling class, at which he had first made the thing and then slipped it into the handbag of the female sculptor working beside him, with a note suggesting she join him for a Thai takeaway in his Transit, since he wished to seek her opinion as to why Michelangelo had chosen to sculpt David during what was obviously a cold snap. Upon opening her bag, she immediately called the police, but, alerted by the sirens, he had managed to escape, deciding, as he ran, to post the thing to me, rather than destroy what might well turn out to be a priceless work of art. What particularly touched me was his regret that if only he had enrolled in the woodwork class next door he would have been able to stand his ground and claim the thing was a cap-peg. A PS informs me that he has now left Rhyl for Accrington, where, he has heard, there is a unisex Scalextric group.

I wish him better luck than that of the distraught hairdresser who wrote to tell me of his dreadful experience after joining a Wiltshire morris dancing society. I have always been attracted to bells, knees and boomps-a-daisy, he writes, and there was this very dishy blacksmith whom, after we had finished hopping about to bless the harvest, I asked for a foxtrot. He hit me with his stave, and I now walk funny. Do you know of an open-minded philately group? Well, as it happens, I do, though I hesitate to recommend it, having also heard from a Hove dentist who says he has just returned from a meeting at which he managed to swap a distressed penny black for a Mrs Henderson in mint condition. However, while it was a relief, for once, to find a happy hobbyist, I think I shall myself stick to etymology: it may occasionally be uncertain, but that's as dubious as it gets.

Cutting the Mustard

THIS morning, I offer you a straw to grasp at. It is only a very small straw, and – such is the tortuousness that I am about to let us both in for – you may well find it very difficult to grasp; but since recent events have almost certainly led you to believe that there are no straws left at all, I feel it to be worth offering. Especially for those of you reading this while standing on the worst platforms in Europe, waiting for the worst trains in Europe; which, if they ever turn up, will almost certainly contain the worst soccer thugs in Europe, who, the worst education system in Europe having failed them utterly and the worst police service in Europe having failed the rest of us utterly, have got on board with the sole object of duffing you up and stealing the mobile phone via which you were just about to tell someone you were finally on the train and with average luck would now be with them on Friday night. Although you won't, of course, because you will have been duffed up so badly as to be left bleeding on a wonky hospital trolley waiting for the worst health service in Europe to get around to misdiagnosing you so that you can be offloaded to what are bound to be the worst funeral parlours in Europe. So – particularly if, as you read, you are simultaneously wondering how it is that we seem to have ended up with the worst Royal Family in Europe – here is your very small straw. Grasp at it.

Now, those of you with even more time on your hands – when, say, you were sitting in traffic jams earlier this morning on the worst roads in Europe, trying to find a contraflow system that would eventually allow you to leave your vehicle to be vandalised in the car park of the station where the worst trains in Europe were not turning up – may have been pondering, now that the word Delia has passed into the *Oxford English Dictionary*, how that word will be translated when the next edition of the Larousse French Dictionary appears. Will it, as you suspect, be *"la pire cuisine de l'Europe"*?

Well, no, it won't. I know this, because I also know four other things: I know that before the new LFD appears on the shelves, those shelves will have been occupied for some months by the French edition of Delia's *How To Cook*. and I know that Messrs Larousse will therefore not dare to slag off a woman whom the French will by then have taken unanimously to their hearts. Which will have very little to do with her cooking. It will have everything to do with the third thing I know, which is that Norwich City FC, whose most illustrious director is, famously, Delia Smith, plays at Carrow Road, and that for more than a century Carrow Road has been very close indeed to all those French hearts poised to have Delia unanimously taken to them.

Not – hang on to that straw, I thought I saw it slip just then – that the French are fans of the Canaries: what they are fans of is something else from Carrow – something which also, coincidentally, turns out in bright yellow, both on its tin and inside, for Carrow is where the Colman's Mustard factory stands. Climb up to its roof, and you can watch the footie, across the river, for free. And, as if being a neighbour of Colman's were not enough, Delia has, in *How To Cook*, not merely identified it as "the one and only home-grown English spice", but turned decorous cartwheels in praise of its supremacy over all other mustards.

Hang about, you cry, are you telling us that French readers, of all people, will, as soon as they spot that ringingly chauvinist plug, take Delia to their Anglophobic hearts? Yes, that is exactly what I am telling you, for we have reached the fourth thing I know: which is that Colman's Mustard is the only English foodstuff ever to have received the Legion d'honneur. Take down your own tin, now (oh, all right, when you train home again on Thursday week) and you will be able not only to corroborate this remarkable gustatory snippet, but also to learn that the same Norwich condiment waltzed off with the gold medal at the 1878 Paris Exhibition, wiping the floor with Meux and Louit, Gray-Poupons and Maille, and all the other weedy Frog mustards which dared to climb in the ring with it. Quite how mustards are judged, I cannot guess – did wax-moustachioed *hommes serieux* in frock coats and silk hats really sit at long tables, tasting and spitting until their mouths puckered to terminal numbness? But however it came about, come about is exactly what it did, and which Frenchman today would compromise his patriotism by failing to applaud Delia's culinary nous in praising a little yellow tin that had been kissed on both cheeks by the President of France?

For being, grasp that straw, the best mustard in Europe.

Paper Money

FOR a hack, getting started is the hardest bit. The first sheet of blank paper is a nightmare. You put it in your typewriter and stare. For a labrador, however, getting started is the easiest bit. The first sheet of blank paper is a doddle. You put it in your mouth and run.

Thereafter, everything becomes less of a nightmare for the hack and less of a doddle for the dog. As sheet follows sheet for the hack, things fall more and more into place, but as sheet follows sheet for the dog, things fall more and more out of place – lamps are tumbled, jugs spilt, cushions scattered, tables unlaid, babies trussed. Because, while the hack uses only three sheets and each is separate, the labrador uses 249 sheets and each is connected: from which you – being quicker on the uptake than both hack and dog – will have by now deduced that the hack works for *The Times*, and the labrador works for Andrex.

Or did. For the nation's most cherished bog-roll has just changed its name. Better yet, it has also changed its paper, and, for me, the most important consequence of this is that life has become slightly less arduous for the labrador. Because, since the new paper is bulkier but the roll is the same size, the labrador has only 241 sheets to run with now, which means that, each sheet being 124mm long, the dog needs to gallop a 992mm shorter distance than it used to. Practically a metre. Or, in dog-life terms, seven metres less running-time, which may now be devoted to leisure, family, friends, and charitable works.

Did I, back there, imply that there was also a least important consequence to the Andrex namechange? Yes, I did: the least important consequence is that life has also become slightly less arduous for people. I know this, because I have spoken to Kimberley-Clark, the creators of the born-again Andrex, who assured me that the new product was even easier to use: it was a "state-of-the-art toilet tissue".

Now, Churchillians among you may be tempted to cry "Some art! Some state!", given what we are talking about when one gets right down to it (as, indeed, one does), but Kimberley-Clark have every right to love their work and the mission to which it is devoted, and when they tell me that I will notice that the new generation of bumf is not only thicker and more absorbent but also softer and gentler on the skin, I have to admire its selfless commitment, even though I personally do not give a . . .

So let me instead come to what I do give one about. It is

14

the new Andrex name – or, rather, the three new names – because, never mind what the stuff inside does for mankind, those names will only make life incalculably more arduous. For it is a very long time indeed since the days when I would sidle sheepishly into a chemist's shop, wait for a male assistant, and, as the hot blood flooded into my peach-fuzzed cheeks, mumble what it was that I wanted; but those days, I fear, are back. That is because the three new names of the Andrex lavatory paper range are: Hold Me and Touch Me and Feel Me. When I asked Kimberley-Clark how they had arrived at this literally unspeakable titling, I was given to understand that it was all a matter of user-friendliness; that was also why they had introduced a yet kindlier version, called Aloe Vera Toilet Tissue. Yes, forgive me, I could not resist agreeing that if your name was Vera you might well warm to a bog-paper that greeted you personally, but their only response was to explain to me – with that po-faced delivery one tends to find in those appointed to supply lavatory rolls to our gracious Queen – that the product not only contained this aloe vera stuff, whatever it is, but was also equipped with soft ripples "to give you an extra level of care".

So then, here I am in Boots, standing at the counter, clearing my throat, summoning the cool wherewithal to ask for six rolls of Hold Me. "We've run out of Hold Me," says the young woman I am desperately trying not to look at, "would Feel Me do?" The woman behind me in the queue says: "I've never heard of them, is there a difference, what does Feel Me do that Hold Me doesn't?" I offer her a shrug, a lop-sided grin, I mutter to the assistant: "Yes, great, fine, Feel Me, half a dozen, jolly good." She turns and hollers: "Mrs Wainwright, can I have six of them Feel Me for this gentleman – hang on," she turns back, "we just got this new one in with soft ripples to give you an extra level of..."

But she is talking to thin air. I am out of there. I am walking down the high street, at a military clip. Somebody, somewhere, must still have a few rolls of Bronco in stock. You knew where you were with that, even if it wasn't fit for a dog.

Combined Operations

THROW open your window this morning and you will hear a nationwide chorus of the *Ode to Joy* welling up from countless NHS trolleys, broom cupboards, lavatory cubicles, hat-racks and wheelie bins, as Britain's crumbling patients give grateful thanks for a Europe which has stepped in to minister to their myriad ills. They are to be sent abroad for treatment. Yet even as the rapturous anthem swells, do we not detect in it the odd wobble of trepidation? Of course we do, for this is Britain, and that is Europe, and old uneasinesses are slow to ebb; what, the afflicted begin to wonder as their sing-song fades, are European medics like?

Fortunately, I know a bit about this. Take, for example, Dutch nurses: these consist of two main types, the tubby, jolly, red-faced Edams, and the thinner, paler, gloomier

Goudas. Both, however, are equally swift to respond to emergencies, since they whizz around the wards on bicycles, although when they dismount, drowsing patients may be startled by the clatter of clogs. Uniquely in European medicine, they are assisted by small boys, who, in the event of stitches suddenly bursting, will poke a finger in the hole until senior help arrives.

Hospital administration in Italy is possibly the most efficient in Europe. In the agricultural south, medical services come under the jurisdiction of a network of local land authorities, called the Mafia, and in the industrial north, they are run by a nexus of interlocked corporations, called the Mafia. Occasionally, you will see a consultant lean over a bed and kiss a patient: the bad news is that the patient hasn't paid up front, the good news is that his bed will soon be vacant. Since your bill is being paid by H M Government, have no worries on that score, unless you wake up in the night to find a horse's head in your bed. It means Mr Milburn's cheque has bounced, and you must phone him immediately.

Surgery in Denmark is excellent, its only drawback being that you will find upon waking up that the word DANISH has been indelibly stencilled on your ribs, from hip to armpit. Try, mind, to avoid a thin glum surgeon who wears black, carries a smelly old skull, and talks to himself a lot: he may never get around to performing your operation.

Avoid Belgium altogether. Since it is the most densely populated country in Europe, shortage of space means that operations are performed with the patients standing up. They are then winched aloft to recover in hammocks. There is also a risk that you will have a French-speaking surgeon and a Flemish-speaking theatre sister: the risk is not that they won't understand one another (they will), but that they won't talk to one another at all. Hospital food consists entirely of sprouts.

You would be on much safer ground in neighbouring Luxembourg. Since time began, Luxembourgeois have been engaged in the nation's only industry, stamp manufacture. In consequence, they have the tiny deft fingers of master perforators, and their micro-surgery is the best in the world. You will also feel less post-operative pain, due to having been not stitched, but gummed. Luxembourg is a small country (in summer, when its tree is in leaf, you can easily drive straight past it), but it does boast two tiny hospitals: I recommend the Stanley Gibbons Infirmary, especially if you have something rare.

France, in contrast, is the largest country in Europe, a great boon for drunks, who need plenty of room to fall. Despite their fabled passion for the grape, however, many French doctors are highly competent, and even after two lunchtime magnums of Burgundy and a tankard of Pernod usually have little trouble in deploying their favourite implement, the suppository; certainly by the third attempt. If, however, your doctor arrives at your bedside with a string of onions round his neck instead of a stethoscope, you would be well advised to seek a second opinion. Be prepared, though, to hear that, after long discussion with your own doctor, the second opinion is that Château Petrus '47 is preposterously overrated.

Which brings me, as you yourself may soon be brought, to Germany, which has both brilliant young surgeons and experienced old ones: the former have lights on their hats, the latter have spikes. Their common fault is that they are prone to an overenthusiastic surgical technique: once inside the patient, they find it almost impossible not to extend their operation. This technique is called *Lebensraum*, and often results in more *Raum* than *Leben*. Should this happen, your relatives would find it fruitless to sue, since the entire staff will claim that they had no idea what was going on and were merely carrying out orders.

What's Your Poison?

BECAUSE this column is even more than usually not what a column should be, I have an apology to make. The apology is not mine, it comes from a sea-urchin, which, for a variety of reasons, cannot make it personally. I am making it on its behalf: I am *in loco Echinus*. You will say, hallo, you seem a bit close to this sea-urchin, to which I will reply, you do not know the half of it. One half of it is that if I had not been a bit close to this sea-urchin, I should not have had to apologise on its behalf, and the other half of it is that although I am now a long way from this sea-urchin, I am still a bit close to it, because of the Manchester scorpion.

For, despite the fact that the sea-urchin is Turkish and the scorpion Mexican, they have much in common. You may already know about the scorpion, if, like me, you were lying with your foot up, listening to the *Six O'Clock News* last Saturday: the scorpion had flown into Manchester from Mexico earlier that day, in the coat pocket of a woman. The woman did not know the scorpion was there, otherwise she would not have put her hand in the pocket, and the scorpion would not have stung her. For which we must not, since this is 2001, blame the scorpion: it is no joke making a ten-hour flight in a hot fluffy pocket, no light, no food, no kip, only to have a big fat five-legged white thing suddenly dive on to you from nowhere. You and I would have lashed out, too. Which of course explains why the BBC – now, in Mr Dyke's gentle hands, more fashionably tender than ever – chose to report the news as it did: for while listeners heard nothing of the hapless stingee's condition, whereabouts, or even name, we were reassured that the stowaway had been carried by RSPCA carers to the home of a scorpion specialist, who, finding it to be distressed and dehydrated, was not only spraying it regularly with water to relieve both, but also contacting even more specialist specialists in a bid to discover its identity, favourite diet, and – who knows? – whether it crawled into the pocket by chance or was in fact seeking asylum from an oppressive Mexican regime which had trodden on thousands of its kin during a brutal campaign of entomological cleansing.

Hallo, you will say again, never mind the scorpion, what was he doing with his foot up of a Saturday, when he should have been at the Benson & Hedges Final, watching Surrey trash Gloucester? That is because you did not see the foot: had you done so, you would not only have appreciated why it could not have been hobbled on to Lord's, you might also have been moved to inquire (since it was nude) why it appeared to be equipped with four toes and a plum. Whereupon I would have replied that I had no idea, yesterday it was merely four toes and a damson, and a couple of days before that, when I flew home from Turkey, it was just five normal toes and a throb.

The throb had been there ever since, earlier in the week, I had trodden on something on the bed of the Aegean, in the course of wading ashore from a boat aboard which I was spending a fortnight with a few convivial chums. We had gone there in an attempt finally to unfathom, quite literally, the ancient mystery of why Homer had described the sea as wine-dark, but in the event the solution was a doddle – it transpires that as a boat pitches in the heavy swell, anything you may be striving to knock back while hanging on to the rail with your other hand can easily slop overboard – so we refocused our attention on less academic pleasures, such as swimming ashore to buy more stuff to replace what was going into either us or the billowing metaphor. And it was on one such expedition that I put my foot down and went Ow.

Do I sense that, in the matter of yoking the two heterogeneous elements of today's rambling folderol together, you are there before me? On Monday, by which time I had four toes and an aubergine, I was ported round to a man with a white coat and a toolbox who removed something which he identified as a sea-urchin spine, and filled the hole with antibiotics, which I identify as the reason this column, in its febrile meanderings, is even more than usually not what a column should be. Having been relieved of one painful problem, however, I have, thanks to the Manchester scorpion, only gained another: in this compassionate world of ours, should I not at least make the attempt to reunite the sliver of urchin with its distant body? It presently lies on my desk, but should I not pop it into an envelope, post it to the captain of our boat (who knows where the amputee languishes, pining for its spine), and bid him commission as deft a micro-surgeon as Turkey boasts, at whatever cost?

It would seem to be the right and proper thing to do, these days.

Soft Noodles

THE Devil makes work for idle hacks. Not that I had intended to be idle last Saturday, I had intended to go to the tennis at the Queen's Club to cheer on Tiny Tim, but – for all that God blesses us, every one – the Devil had been up to his old tricks there, too, and the rain was drumming on the covers so thunderously that even if Queen's had been staging the Stella Artois Water Polo Tournament, it would have been called off. So I stayed home and switched on Trooping the Colour, where the poor bloody infantry were yomping up and down in four acres of knee-high puddle, bringing on the unsettling thought that if one of them fainted, as they are sometimes wont to do, the torrent might take his rigid supine form and wash it right out of Horseguard's Parade, down the Mall, and into some Whitehall drain, just like Hans Christian Andersen's constant tin soldier; and because this image not surprisingly brought a tear to my eye, and

I'd had quite enough superfluous water for one day, I switched off the box. Whereupon the Devil saw to it that I picked up *The Times*.

Which, on page four, carried a photograph of a new-born bongo. However, despite being the greatest newspaper in the world, *The Times* did not say what a bongo was. It said only that the new bongo was called Noodles, and that its father, an old bongo, also shown in the photograph, was called Ali. This, as the Devil knew it would, irritated me no end: not only did I not know what a bongo was, other than that it was an animal of some kind, any fool could see that, I did not know why the London Zoo, where the new one was born three weeks ago, should have christened it Noodles; I could, of course, take a shy at why the zoo had christened its father Ali, because I recalled a great magician called Ali Bongo whom I had seen with my own father, not called Ali, at the Finsbury Park Empire in 1947, where he wore a fez, not my father, and, among other things, vanished a girl with terrific legs from his wardrobe, possibly because Mrs Bongo had just walked in downstairs, I can't tell you for sure, I was only nine; so I assume that whoever is in charge of christenings at the London Zoo saw the act, too, and charmingly wished to pay Mr Bongo the homage he so richly deserves. Noodles Bongo is, however, another matter entirely. Is it, perhaps, a gourmet dish in its native land – wherever that is when it isn't Regent's Park – in which case the Christening Dept. has a pretty tacky sense of humour? Or could it be that Ali Bongo, the other one, the one in the fez, had a son called Noodles, and the zoo was simply being consistent? I stared out of the window. The rain came down. Time passed. And eventually, of course, the Devil said: go on, phone.

So I did, and after pushing a lot of star buttons and listening to a lot of compelling stuff about foot-and-mouth and banqueting and cut-price videos and how to adopt a pelican, I finally made contact with a human being in a peaked cap (you can tell, I swear) and I said: "I believe you have a new bongo", and he said: "Yes, we have", and I said: "Can I come and see it?" and he said: "Yes, you'll find it in the Old Cattle House", so at least I now knew, roughly, what a bongo was, though why Noodles wasn't in the New Cattle House I couldn't imagine, unless it was because bongos like to stay with their dads for a bit, until they are old enough to be told what to do if they find a good-looking female bongo in their wardrobe.

Now, the London Zoo is just a toddle from where I live, now that I have left the Old Cricklewood House, so I put my brolly up and sloshed across the park, and I paid my tenner, and I sought out the Old Cattle House, and there were the bongos, père et fils. There was also a keeper. "Is that Noodles?" I said. "Yes," he said. We were both, by the way, grown men. "Why is it called Noodles?" I asked. "Hard to say," he replied. "There's a committee." So I came home again.

But the Devil had not yet finished with me. When I picked up *The Times* once more to check on the bongos – to whom I had now grown close – I spotted that the self-same page contained this short item: "The Prince of Wales attended one of the country's only agricultural shows to be held this summer but because of foot-and mouth disease there were no cattle at the East of England Show in Peterborough. The only cow was a giant inflatable canvas one which collapsed in the wind." Is it not at times like this that one's heart truly goes out to HRH? All the way to Peterborough in the pouring rain just to see a canvas cow go bang, when you and I, unbound by the exigencies of duty and high office, can stroll across Regent's Park any old time we like, and see a living bongo.

Poles Apart

THERE are some 12 million married couples in Britain, and I am confident that Mrs Coren and I speak for all of them when I say we are flabbergasted at the hysterical adulation currently being lavished on Mr and Mrs Thornewill. We are flummoxed; we are gobsmacked; we are stumped; and, yes, we are not a little gutted. We cannot for the life of us understand what all the fuss is about. Why are Mr and Mrs Thornewill being lionised and feted, simply for becoming the first married couple to walk to the North Pole?

What kind of achievement is that? To walk to the North Pole, you point the compass at the horizon and put one foot after the other. There being neither roads nor car, one spouse does not have to read the map while the other spouse drives; there is no risk of yelling, grabbing, chucking maps out of windows while swerving dangerously, or turning this bloody thing round right now and going straight home, it wasn't my idea to come in the first place. Nor, as night falls, is anybody sitting in the middle of nowhere interrogated as to why they didn't have the sense to fill up when they had the chance, or invited to explain in words of one syllable why they won't stop and ask someone the way, since there is no one to ask, unless you speak bear. As for finding mutually satisfactory overnight accommodation, transarctic spouses do not have to run in and out of a dozen hotels to find a room one of them neglected to book in advance, or end up sleeping foetally on the back seat while drunks widdle on their bumpers; transarctic spouses have a folding nylon hotel on their little sled, and when they are tucked up snugly inside it and fancy dinner, they do not go nuts trying to catch the waiter's eye or ringing a room-service voicemail that never rings back, they simply pop a bubble-pack and chomp on a nourishing pellet that tastes of nothing requiring comment. Neither of them orders a second bottle when they know what it does to them, your father was the same, nor do they engage in stand-up rows about toenails in the bidet or hairs on the soap.

Upon arrival at the North Pole, no married couple will suffer recriminatory disappointment. Of course it is not finished. It is not even started. There is no lying ratbag of a manager to wave a brochure at, there are no rooms better than the one they thought they'd booked, and the swimming pool is a reproachless umpteen miles across, albeit solid. Neither spouse will find the place infuriatingly classier or tackier than the other had led them to believe: the clothes they stand up in will be absolutely perfect, because, if they try to change into anything else, they will not be standing up for much longer, they will turn blue, topple, and snap.

Polar couples do not bicker about what to do during the day, either: shopping, scuba-diving, sightseeing, paragliding, gambling, visiting the doll museum, lying by the pool staring at that woman, I wasn't staring, and so forth, are unavailable for marital dispute. What polar couples do during the day is walk. They do not even have the option of standing still. If one of them stands still for more than a few seconds, he or she becomes a permanent topographical feature. Nor are they required to argue nightly about whose turn it is to get up at the crack of dawn and bag a lounger: any territorial claims that German couples might have entertained about the Arctic Riviera have so far proved to be atypically muted, and while there must always be a chance that, some day, Herr und Frau Jerry will be sprinting out six months before sun-up to begin oiling one another at minus 60 degrees, it was not, as I understand it, a problem for the Thornewills.

But did this first mould-breaking couple run, as so many of Britain's other 12 million have run, the risk of holiday boredom? Unlikely: while there are, admittedly, precious few topics of Arctic conversation, all of them white, no couple can manage more than two seconds of speech before tugging their balaclavas back up, lest their lips go solid and chip off. Since most duologue therefore consists of waving mittens about, the likelihood of vacational chat occasioning marital ennui is remote; unless, of course, one of the Thornewills was a semaphore freak.

In short, their chilly stroll was a doddle from start to

finish. I was not in the least surprised when Fiona hugged Mike and confided to the phalanx of goggling hacks that "the trip has brought us much closer together. I really want to encourage other couples so that they too can achieve their lifetime's dreams." Bang on the money, Mrs Thornewill: look for me and Mrs Coren this very weekend, and you will find us shopping at Sleds 'R' Us.

Not My Bag

Had you, last week, been taking a sundown stroll through the rolling Bucks verdure, you might have spotted a strange misshapen silhouette blemishing the evening horizon, rooted to a hummock. A stunted oak? A Saxon rood? An extravagant horse-dropping, piled and eroded by the summer wind? Or even, perhaps, a statue of Charles Laughton, raised by the Gerrards Cross Victor Hugo Society? That fearsome hump, those twisted legs, the shoulder dropping to the wonky knee as the agonised head wrenches unnaturally upward, poking its pitiful eye at the uncaring heavens – what could it be but the great hunchback himself, frozen forever by the sculptor's art?

It could be a wag practising his golf-swing, is what. That the figure displayed not a tremor of movement is explained by its having been swinging for three hours and finally come to a paralysed halt. Had some

Samaritan not karted by, I might have been there yet, a topographical conundrum fit to rank with Stonehenge and the White Horse of Uffington. For the world would not know that the reason I was there was only because a malign joker had bought me, for my birthday, golf lessons. And I had just learnt them all.

Here is the first: if God had wanted man to play golf, He would have given him an elbowless left arm, short asymmetrical legs with side-hinged knees, and a trapezoid rib-cage from which diagonally jutted a two-foot neck topped by a three-eyed head. Here is the second: since the game can be played only by grotesquely distorting the body God did give us, golf was patently invented by manufacturers. For the natural way to play golf would be to throw the ball down the fairway, walk after it, pick it up and throw it again, and, having reached the green, throw it down the hole. However, in some distant eon, a chippie of fortuitous ineptitude whittled a cabriole leg a foot longer than the rest and, rather than write it off as a tax loss, decided to concoct a use for it. He then drew up a list of things you could not do, such as throw the ball, and an industry was born, with the game as a sideline, where the profit was limitless, provided you made the game constantly trickier. That is why 17 more holes were added, all so different as to require the industry to sell you as many different clubs, and when even these yielded inadequate profits, go out with shovels and dig bunkers, which led to a whole new species of club, and even more painful and humiliating contortion. No surprise that Hitler committed suicide in one.

With all these clubs and a body misshapen by their

demands, man was clearly in no state to drag the stuff around, allowing a caring industry to ply him not only with bags, trolleys and karts, but with special shoes to tether him to the ground while swinging his ruins about, and special gloves to stop the clubs blistering his hands, and distinctively garish trousers to offset (inadequately) the risk of other golfers felling him, and 189 books called *Improve Your Swing*, which don't, because the industry wants you to buy the 190th.

Yet, having worked all this out as I stood rooted on my very first round, it struck me that I could have got it all wrong. Might God have wanted man to play golf, after all? Did He, sitting back on the seventh day, say: I'll call it Sunday, and I'll give them golf. They will all start imperfect, and I shall send them out with their imperfections, and I shall give them all manner of hazards along the way, and if improving touches them with pride, I shall make them worse; they will have days of joy, and days of despair, and each will test them after its own fashion, and from time to time I shall people the earth with saints like Hogan and Nicklaus and Woods, to set examples and to point the way of Truth, and the authorised version of My laws shall be constantly revised, to keep them on the hop, so that Man, and Woman that is born of Man, shall trudge the courses of the earth in fair weather and in foul, and be tested at every tree and rough and bog and bit that lies a foot outside the railings, and – just when things are looking up – dumb caddies shall poke an illegal 15th club into their bags to drive them nuts, and though they can never be perfect, it is in their striving that they shall become good.

More yet: even as Mrs Coren lowered me into the tub that

30

night and went off giggling to broach the liniment, it occurred to me that perhaps Elysium might be nothing but a wondrous golf course, where the eternal day was free alike of hail or crosswind, and where we shall all be reborn with short rubber legs and straight left arms and all the other boons divinely withheld from us on Earth, and our swings shall all be perfect and all our putts plumb-straight. Either that, or you won't stand an earthly, or rather, a heavenly, of getting in if you're anything less than scratch; and, even then, you'll have to know Somebody. In which case, I may have left it a bit late, on both counts.

Road Rage

L AST night, at the Camden Odeon, bang in the middle of *Bridget Jones's Diary*, I got my old trouble back. I hadn't had my old trouble for nearly 40 years. I last got it at the Swiss Cottage Odeon, bang in the middle of *Dr No*. You will say, aha, his old trouble clearly has something to do with Ursula Andress wriggling out of her rubber bikini, that would explain why it came back last night, it was on account of Renée Zellweger wriggling out of her rubber knickers, I rather think we have the measure of Mr Coren's old trouble, do we not – but you are wrong. While it is true that my old trouble is about cinema distraction, when some minor feature suddenly lurches the mind away from the major feature and strands it in an obsessional limbo while the major feature spools on unnoticed, it has nothing to do with snappy latex, or even snappy women. What it has everything to do with is snappy cars.

Now, quiz most filmgoers about James Bond's motor and they will begin rabbiting on about the Aston Martin which could deploy greater firepower than Nato while catapulting undesirable hitch-hikers through its roof. That is because they have forgotten 007's first car. It was a Sunbeam Alpine. I have not forgotten, because I had one, too. I had driven to *Dr No* in it in 1962, but it was getting on for 1963 by the time I got there, because the Swiss Cottage Odeon was at the top of Belsize Road, a 1 in 45 gradient, and the Alpine was the slowest sports car in the world. Which was why, a scant few minutes into the film, my old trouble came on: when Bond got into his Alpine, I did not see the exemplar of butch chic which product placement wanted me to see. I saw a gullible dork who had recently driven out of his local Rootes showroom leaving cackling salesmen rolling about on the floor. Things grew worse when, a little later, Bond effortlessly eluded the doctor's thugs in a highspeed car chase: an Alpinist myself, I knew that, had the arch-villain been not Dr No but United Dairies, their milk-float would have caught Bond within 50 yards. This was a bogus film, with a bogus hero, and, for the remainder of it, I could concentrate on nothing else: when Ursula Andress splashed out of the surf, it might as well have been Thora Hird.

I flogged my doddering Alpine soon after that to some Bondabee sucker, and bought an Austin-Healey 3000. A true sports car: had weedy Bond got in and turned the engine on, he would probably have fainted at the thunder. And every film it appeared in got the casting right: it was always driven by a raffish cove with wrists of steel and a bulldog briar. Never a twinge of my old trouble there. Offscreen, I drove mine with joy until 1969, when I sold it with grief, and bought the car which, last night, did bring on the old trouble again. I had to do that because in 1969 Mrs Coren gave birth to a *Times* columnist, and when I went to collect the pair of them from Queen Charlotte's Hospital, we could squeeze *The Times* columnist's carrycot into the little slot behind the seats only by shoving the seats so far forward that our knees covered our ears. Nor, when it began to rain at Shepherds Bush, could we shut the roof because *The Times* columnist was in the way, so he got wet. It didn't bother him, because he knew he would get at least three paragraphs out of it some day, but it bothered us.

The next day I chopped the Healey in for a secondhand Mercedes 220SEb cabriolet. It was not only the biggest convertible in the world, it was the safest: conceived out of postwar nostalgia for the Tiger tank, it was two tons of iron and walnut, with a three-ply reinforced hood able to protect *The Times* columnist from anything the heavens could chuck at him. For Jerry, it was a snook cocked at the shade of Bomber Harris, but for me it was a rite of passage: I was a family man now, tasked not to boy-race, but to trundle and protect. And that is why, last night, the old trouble came back.

In *Bridget Jones's Diary*, Hugh Grant plays a cad. We do not know he is a cad, though, until he takes the cuddly eponym off for a lively weekend; and the egregious signifier of his caddishness is his car. An autobuff's veteran one-off that gives the finger to the common Ferrari or Porsche, it is patently a Flash Harry's car; for that is what 30 years have done to the Mercedes 220SEb cabriolet. It irritated me no end; it ruined the film; it left the second half unnoticed. I just sat there thinking: this car was not put on earth so that smirking jerks could pull dippy women, it was given to us so that solid men could poddle invulnerably through the traffic with *The Times* columnist and his sister the *Observer* poker correspondent on the back seat, punching one another and shouting: "Dad, Dad, are we there yet, Dad?"

Wink in the Willows

I DID *not read that University of Wisconsin study analysing the relationship between feminism and male homosexuality. Did Kenneth Grahame, though?*

The Mole had been working very hard all morning, spring-cleaning his little home. It was the way he thought of it, these days.

When he first married Mrs Mole he thought of it as her little home. He would go off to work, thinking: that is my wife in her little home. It felt good; it felt masculine. At work, quarrying beside the other titchy navvies, or at lunch breaks where they would spit the grit from their molars and chat convivially over a shared woodlouse, he would refer to Mrs Mole as his better half or the trouble-and-strife, thereby establishing his credentials in the marital club and enabling him to swap jokes and anecdotes with fellow members. The jokes, of course, were libellous, the anecdotes untrue, but this never bothered them: all females, however beloved, were comic grist.

It was in the third month of their marriage that things took a strange turn: the Mole had been looking forward to coming home to an evening with his paws up, a gourmet meal filling his little gut, and starting a family, when instead he found a silent hole littered with the day's droppings, and a note informing him that his worm was in the floor. Angrily, he dug it up; glumly, he ate it; bitterly, he waited for Mrs Mole to return and explain herself.

She arrived at midnight. "I have been at a seminar on breast-feeding," Mrs Mole said, "and the politics of sexual enslavement. We in our new Riverbank Sisterhood Committee have decided to wean any future offspring onto little grubs at the earliest opportunity, so's we can get out and fulfil our destinies. The breast is an iron ball shackled to the ankle of female liberty."

The Mole gaped. After a bit, he said: "All right, answer me this, if God had wanted you to feed 'em little grubs, why'd he give you eight nipples?"

She did not answer. She did not, indeed, say anything more that night, except: "Don't start that!"

She was up early next morning. "You'll have to get your own breakfast," she said. "I'm off to work."

"You what?"

"I do not consider pushing your droppings down the tunnel and ensuring you get fresh worms of an evening to be the role for which I was ordained. We only pass this way but once. I am going into the interior decorating business with Ms Toad. Independence is the name of the game."

And so it proved to be. With the accelerating success of Toadmole Decor, the Moles saw less and less of one another; especially after Ms Mole's raging ambition inevitably sought the wider political arena, where she marched, picketed, lobbied and rose to such iconic status that when she threw up a molehill at Tattenham Corner, causing the Queen's Derby favourite to trail in fourth, even the broadsheets made it their front-page splash.

All of which served only to deepen the despair of the hapless Mole: his workmates, excluding him from the jolly cut-and-thrust of marital chaff, now inquired solicitously about his dishpan paws and soufflé recipes, before collapsing hysterically beside their half-dug mounds. So he gave up work and sat all winter among the detritus of mouldy worms and old, dried droppings.

And then spring came to the riverbank. Which was why the Mole, lacking any other means of responding to the seasonal urges that stirred within him, had been working very hard all morning, spring-cleaning his little home — until he could take no more. Scraping with his little claws and muttering "Up we go! Up we go!" he tunnelled his way out and found himself rolling in the warm grass. He sat up, and looked across the river, and suddenly, in a dark hole in the bank, he saw something. It winked at him, and so declared itself to be an eye. Then a face began to grow around it – a little brown face, with whiskers, small neat ears, silky hair and a roguish twinkle.

"Hello, sailor!" the Water Rat said.

"Hello," the Mole said. "I'm not a sailor, though."

"I didn't think you were," Rattie giggled. "I saw you doing all that cheeky rolling about and I said to myself, that's never a sailor, I bet that's never even *been* on a boat, I bet that's just *dying* for a go on my boat, I said."

"Are boats nice?" the Mole asked, suddenly feeling inexplicably odd.

"Are boats *nice*?" shrieked the Rat. "Believe me dear, there is nothing, absolutely nothing, half so much worth doing as simply messing about in boats."

"What do you mean," the Mole asked, "messing about?"

The Water Rat smiled. "Hang on," he murmured, "and I'll get the boat."

Where There's A Wills

Do not fear for the Next-But-Once And Future King. Do not lie sleeplessly worrying whether the long pink boy has too short a cot, do not gnaw your fretful knuckle about his diet or his libido or his laundry or his bicycle or his hangovers, or even about the pulsing zit on his noble conk, do not shred your neurones over his missing saucepan or his ramshackle essay on Vincent van Breughel, for he is in safe hands. He has someone to watch over him.

I know this because I myself, 27 years ago this selfsame

week, became a member of St Andrews University. Now, you will glance at the wizened features on my dust jacket, tot up on your fingers, and say it must have taken him 30 years to get the requisite A-levels, no surprises there, but you are wrong: I did not go to St Andrews as an undergraduate, I went as the Rector. Why the students voted me in I can never know, but merely surmise that it was because of the alternatives: the late (though not then) Sir Nicholas Fairbairn, whose notoriously bizarre habits were clearly too ripe even for undergraduate tastes, and Sir (though not then) Jackie Stewart, who had just retired from the Grand Prix circuit and may therefore have been perceived by the electorate as a wimp, when compared with a man for whom even the Hangar Lane gyratory system held no terrors.

Thus I found myself, in the autumn of 1974, standing on the Nook of Fife, albeit not vertically, but leaning into the wind and flapping, much in the manner of Marcel Marceau; because in St Andrews it was not the autumn of 1974, it was still the winter of 1831, which began on June 15 that year, after the Nook's last mild day. For – if you are not familiar with nooks, believing them to be much like crannies – you should know that the Fife one is the coldest in the world, and though it also has the best beaches in the world, they can be crossed only by dog-sled. That first night I stayed in a charming little hotel with John Cleese, the outgoing Rector, and since it was so chill in our rooms, we huddled downstairs boozing for warmth, until Cleese got drunk enough to ask the proprietor if he would ignite the central heating, and the proprietor said we were the only guests and he wasn't switching on the boiler for just two wee rooms, d'ye no have scarves? The next morning, an inspired Cleese rushed home to start scribbling *Fawlty Towers*, but I had to stay on, because I was the Rector, and I had responsibilities, now. I had 3,000 chapped and shivering charges to cosset.

It is because St Andrews undergraduates live in permafrost that they are so often glum, and it is because they are so often glum that they need a Rector. Especially since St Andrews is also the farthest university from anywhere, with the exception of Mars Polytechnic, and as tiny as it is isolated: the town has three streets, a golf course, and a crumbly sea wall which the entire student body ritually stumbles along each week, wearing their uniquely thick woolly gowns to mitigate the blizzard, risking life and limb as they pitifully scan for a ship which might take them back to civilisation. It is the Rector's duty to represent that civilisation: he is an emissary from the real world, where he has knocked about a bit, and knows stuff, whereas they have been plucked from that world, as yet knowing no stuff at all, and dumped in fairyland. So, every month, I would trek the unbeaten track to the Nook and spend a couple of days holding surgeries to which distraught youth would flock for succour, in the hope of an even break.

They worried about everything, but could cope with nothing. They wanted to know if they were going mad, or if I could get them a curtain, or how you cured thrush, or if they were allowed to keep a cat, or how much drink is too much drink, or whether they would get their grant docked for cheating, or did I think they should have the baby, or should they change subjects/rooms/religion/sex, would I speak to their tutor, their mother, their priest, their doctor, their bank-manager...

I can't say how well the system worked, they will all be pushing 50 now, I cannot know how many are drunk or catless or old women who were once young men, but it seemed a pretty good system at the time. That time has changed, students are streetwiser now, St Andrews is twice the size and connected to the mains, but that does not stop me feeling reassured that, should a long pink boy feel the need to tap on a far oak door to ask who you go to for a new bath-plug, or whether Jock McFalstaff is a bad influence, or what Christmas present you buy a grannie who has everything, he has a deeply caring gentle soul to soothe, advise, and ministrate. He has a Rector. He has Andrew Neil.

Horsepower

How wonderful that our great leader has appointed Baroness Hayman as Minister for Horses! Like him, I cannot think of a better alternative to an integrated transport policy. So, since millions of you will now be eager to show your gratitude by swopping your car for a horse but not know where to begin, I have decided to cobble together a few simple guidelines for those to whom a horse has hitherto been nothing more than a nasty moment in a Belgian bistro.

Many of you, of course, will already have rejected

the motorcar for the bicycle, often as part of an alternative lifestyle. This is a great mistake. The fact that it is far easier to eat yoghurt or knit a whole-earth poncho on a horse should have alerted alternative livers to the main advantage of the horse over the bicycle, which is that the bicycle is two-dimensional. You cannot shelter beneath it when it rains, and you do not, when shopping, need to lean a horse against Tesco's window. Nor does a horse need to be pumped-up, oiled, or carried indoors at night.

The *ingénu* should not be afraid of buying a horse. It is far less risky than buying a car: a dodgy dealer cannot stuff sawdust into a horse's crank-case, fill its body with plastic padding, or wind its clock back. True, he can disguise certain of its behavioural shortcomings, and the lack of a left lung will not be apparent to the cursory glance, so get a vet to run it round the block. If it cannot outrun the vet, look elsewhere. Do not worry about paddocks: you do not need a large space to keep a horse; remember that before Nigel and Fiona moved into their titchy Knightsbridge mews house, a horse lived there.

However, a horse is undeniably a one-seater, so I'm afraid that family outings will be a thing of the past. There will be no one beside you to point out that it would have been quicker going via Basingstoke, no children behind you gouging one another's eyes out over whose turn it is to be sick on the carpet, no elderly in-laws shrieking what's that funny noise, what's that funny smell, slow down, where are we, don't overtake that milk-float. Sad, but there it is.

Running costs are negligible: no road tax, insurance, MoT or fuel, and should you ever exceed the speed limit, any court expenses may be offset by entering the animal for the Cesarewitch. Hay is not cheap, as our new Minister will attest – the Haymans have been making stacks since 1304 – but at least neither the cost nor the availability of fodder is subject to the whims of Opec or President Saddam Hussein. Horses do, of course, require occasional servicing and repair, but not only is this relatively cheap, it is also unlikely that a vet will squirt a droplet of grease onto your horse's nipples, charge you £397.28 plus VAT, and then disclaim all responsibility when, as you drive away, its leg falls off.

I hear what he says, you may be thinking, but can I drive a horse up a motorway? Fortunately, the law prevents this. Therefore, since the law also prevents you driving a car up a motorway, by placing little red cones across it, you will not be stuck for six hours outside Kegworth while your brain comes to bits. The question you should be asking, since motorways have coneless greensward on either side is: can I gallop a car up a field?

Nevertheless, I appreciate that many car-owners may be worried that when the new initiative has seen to it that fetlocks have at last replaced radials, there will be nothing to talk about when horse-owners foregather at The Rat & Cockle. Fear not! There will be ten times as much to bellow at one another. Just as you once learnt to rabbit on about quick-lift cams, polished ports, ZF differentials and T-head blocks, without really understanding a single word, so you will in the fullness of time learn to drone on interminably about eggbutt snaffles, grackle nosebands, wind-sucking, Irish martingales and numnahs. Remember, too, that you will be breaking things that car-owner may break only once in a lifetime

42

and then too late to talk about. Clavicles, scapulae, vertebrae ribs, femurs and teeth will provide the horseperson with a lifetime of scintillating chit-chat until the day when he finally trots out of the vale of tears behind a brace of appropriately nodding plumes.

All well and good, you say, I can see what an inestimable transport boon Baroness Hayman's inspired appointment could herald, but will there be enough horses in the showrooms to meet the national need? Well, let me put it this way: if it were possible to build vehicles without costly factories, complicated plant, expensive raw materials, overpaid management, militant labour, and foreign blackmail, simply by putting two Vectras into a field and letting them get on with it, do you think Vauxhall would be in the state it is today?

Keep on the Grass

When *The Guinness Book of Coughing* comes to be written, my entry will probably run to several pages. There may even be photographs, some in colour, showing me smoking different things. That is because I have, in my time, smoked every thing there is. I have smoked cigarettes, tipped and untipped, all across the tarry spectrum from neat asphalt to cherry menthol and back again, I have smoked cigars and cigarillos and stogies and cheroots, I have smoked briars and church-wardens and meerschaums and corncobs, variously stuffed with shag and flake and latakia and perique, I have sucked on hubble-bubbles and hookahs and narghiles containing God knows what, and I have done all this since the old century was young.

For as a Boy Scout, I was always prepared: before I rubbed two sticks together, I would first expose the pith with my jack-knife, and upon ignition, pass one stick to Gerald Finch, and we would smoke together. It was good stuff, bamboo. It drew well, it smoked cool, and, after a bit, it did your head in. One moment you were riding along on the crest of a wave, the next you were rolling around in a maelstrom. I got through a lot of bamboo, in the Cockfosters 1374 Troop. Had Baden-Powell dished out badges for smoking, my green pullie would have looked like Goering's white tuxedo.

And there was, of course, bamboo etiquette, because that is the way it is with all smoking. Bamboo smoking was done cross-legged, for safer swooning, it was done communally, behind huts, and when the bamboo had burnt so short that your lips began to fry, the stubs were poked deep into the ground to erase all evidence. Dog-end smoking, however, to which all bamboo smokers graduated, had a different etiquette: stubs covertly collected from parental ashtrays were pooled, dismantled, rolled into tubes of *News Chronicle*, and shared out equally, so that offspring from abstemious homes were not deprived. Smokers are generous folk, because they began that way. Cigarette smokers never lit up without first proffering the pack, pipe smokers always handed you the jar, the pouch, the Turkish slipper, cigar smokers invariably snapped open the humidor so that guests might joyfully reach in for a ten-quid stick. And for those who smoked cannabis, it was done literally on a hand to hand basis. It was a joint activity.

You will have noted the past tense, and you will therefore know where I am coming from. I am coming from a time when smokers did all that, but I have arrived at a time when they do not do that at all. Smoking etiquette has changed: smokers do not proffer a pack now, because before it has cleared their pocket, profferees reel back shrieking and composing their forefingers into a cross. Smokers creep into the garden to wheeze alone. Pipe smokers do not go out anywhere, because they are not let in anywhere. Cigar smokers keep boiled sweets in the humidor, just in case anyone asks them what that big mahogany box is for. Which leaves only one etiquette unchanged: cannabis is still smoked in the old time-honoured way, because when two or three pot-puffers are gathered together, they know exactly why they're there. They do not proffer speculatively, on *terra incognita*, and they are not therefore sneered at, ridiculed, lectured, and shown lurid snapshots of kippered lungs before being chucked out into the sleet.

But, having trudged through the past and present tenses, we have fetched up at the future one, and it stands poised to be more tense than any. For, thanks in no small part to the remarkable Ann Widdecombe (who has startled even her most hysterical critics by pre-emptively driving a wooden stake into her own heart), and the whipping of the hoop by David Blunkett, the day cannot be far off when cannabis is so effectively decriminalised as not only to allow the Shadow Cabinet to cartwheel happily back to one of the less contentious indiscretions of its youth, but also to make the habit *de rigeur* wherever the bogus cool foregather. Trust me, I know about these things, I can remember when monkfish was given only to the cat, I ate polenta when it was semolina, I knew olive oil before it was a virgin.

Cannabis etiquette will change overnight. Flip-top packets of twenty will be downloaded from supermarket shelves into ten million daily pockets and handbags, to be gleefully proffered wherever and whenever. Living-rooms from Land's End to John o'Groats will be full of giggling people wondering why the clock is going backwards. Will this make any difference to me? Fat chance. I shall still be stuck in the bloody garden, on the end of a forbidden Rothman.

The Dirty Half-Dozen

THE seat was for two, but there were seven of us on it. Every other seat was empty, which is the way it can be, upstairs, on a Number 13 bus, in the middle of the afternoon. I always sit upstairs, because I always sat upstairs when you could smoke upstairs, and though you cannot smoke upstairs now, I always haul myself unnecessarily upstairs, just in case, just this once, it will turn out to be a magic bus and I shall get to the top of the steps and find a thick blue fog, and flat-capped men in boots and mufflers with Woodbines jiggling on their lower lips, and schoolboys turning illicitly green.

But I didn't find any of this, yesterday; I found only, when I sat down, six eggs sitting beside me. In, for their safety and comfort, a box. The box had a happy chicken on it, pecking under a sunlit tree, close to a little wooden coop; this was a lucky chicken, it ranged free, it ate what it fancied, and it could therefore knock its kids out at 89p for six. Had the box shown 50 chickens with their heads poking through tin holes, the kids would not have fetched more than 59p, tops. All this was clear: what was not clear was (a) what these well-bred kids were doing, unaccompanied, on the Number 13 bus, and (b) what I should do about them. If they had been abandoned accidentally, should they be handed in, this being a conductorless bus, to the driver? He would not thank me, it had been hard enough persuading him to change a tenner, and anyway, how would I do it? Get off at my stop, run round to the front of the bus, oy, there's a queue, are you wossname or something, so I would wait in the queue, get on the bus, wave the eggs at the driver, I do not open this window for anybody, sunshine, if it cannot be poked through the official slot provided, I do not want to know, you have pissed me about enough already with that tenner, it is only through the goodness of my heart you are not still stood standing at Swiss Cottage, why don't you just take them eggs, one by one, and shove...

But suppose, by a miracle, he opened his window and accepted them: what then? If he were honest and committed them to a lost property office, they would

47

either get addled waiting to be reclaimed, who goes looking for six lost eggs, or, yet more tragically, hatch: six little chicks pecking their way out and finding themselves in some dank hell-hole full of umbrellas and cellphones, no worms, no grain, no caring Clara Cluck; a bad place to die. But if, on the other hand, he were dishonest, kept them, took them home – put the kettle on Elsie, here's a turn-up, I got six top-class eggs off of a prat, where's the toaster, where's the ketchup – mightn't that be worse? Not that I begrudge him either sort of poaching, but if the booty were to kill him, possibly Elsie, too, never mind a couple of kids and the cat who licked the plates, I might be traced, held responsible, arraigned, banged up.

They can do that, eggs. Do not be misled by sell-by dates, listeria is no respecter of franking; besides, who could say with any confidence, these days, that their abandonment had indeed been accidental? The eggs might have been got at by anyone, Omelette Rights activists, the Chicken Wing of the IRA, and planted on the bus to poison and terrorise. If, that is they were eggs at all: they could be explosives, the private bomb has come a long way since it looked like an iron plum pudding with a fuse sticking out, ask anyone, the box could have been left there by a Bin Laden supporter, a Manx nationalist, a Chelsea fan; merely by opening it to have a peek, which I had thoughtlessly done, I might well have triggered one of those titchy time-set detonators you can hide in the dot of an i. The sort of i you find on a "Six Free Range Eggs" label.

The seven of us, however, carried on lurching down Baker Street and none of us went bang. I was nearly at Selfridges, now, I should have to get off in order to address the day's business of buying underpants and two cooked lobsters (unconnected purchases, since you're kind enough to inquire), but what was to be done with my six little chums? Simply leaving them where they were was no answer, in this momentous week of the lovely new Human Rights Act: while mine may not be a household name wherever top Eurojurists foregather, I'm nevertheless prepared to bet that somewhere in the five tonnes of small print there is a sly gobbet about the wilful neglect of unborn chickens which is expressly designed to stick brutes like me on Devil's Island. So when I got off, I went round to the driver's side and told him he had eggs upstairs. "You're the joker with the tenner," he said, and slammed the window. But I should worry: let him do the worrying, now.

Southern Discomfort

Most *Times* readers, I suspect, will not have been nearly as excited as I to spot a tiddly paragraph tucked away in a page 11 cranny of the newspaper's Monday edition. That is because most *Times* readers spend fruitful lives in worthwhile employment, instead of frittering away their brief span staring out of a window and wondering whether they will ever write a blockbuster novel. I, on the other hand, have spent 40 years busting my block in the effort to do exactly that, to no good end: because I cannot come up with a novel, in either sense, plot. On those infrequent occasions when I think I have thought of one, second thoughts serve only to make me think of who thought of it first. Bloody Tolstoy, I think, bloody Smollett.

Or, rather, used to think. Because, since Monday, I have been unable to think of anything but. I am thicker with plots than a Cabinet sauna, thanks to Ms Alice Randall. Here is that paragraph in full: "The estate of Margaret Mitchell is seeking to block publication of a novel that tells *Gone With The Wind* from a slave's perspective. Alice Randall said that her novel *The Wind Done Gone* is an antidote to a text that has hurt generations of Afro-Americans." The woman is a genius: though I do not know whether that genius extends to her writing – the book may be full of scenes showing mobs of enthusiastic spectators high-fiving one another and shouting "Yo!" as Atlanta burns to a frazzle, or Rhett Butler being floored by an expertly swung banjo – frankly, my dears, I don't give a damn. For Alice's true genius lies in the invention of the obverse plot: everything that has hitherto been written can henceforth be rewritten from the other side.

My only problem now is selection. Patently, revisionism will, these days, have to go hand in hand with political rectitude – no publisher would touch *Sophie's Choice* written from Himmler's point of view – but, if anything, that casts my net even wider. Should I take a crack at *Lady Chatterley's Husband*, in which Mellors falls for the bloke in the wheelchair? Or *Ahab the Fishmonger*, written by a tragic hero ("Call me Moby") threatened with extinction at the hands of the catsmeat industry, a bestselling blubber from start to finish? What about *Robinson's Jam*, in which the cannibals, gamely refusing to chuck in the sponge and give up their time-honoured ethnic cuisine, not only barbecue Man Friday but also imaginatively extend their diet to include white meat? Then again, could there ever have been a minor fictional figure more constantly abused, and therefore more deserving of his own 15 minutes, or perhaps seconds, of retributive fame than the eponymous hero of *Portnoy's* ****?

I was juggling all these options and more – having somewhat regretfully rejected *The Chumps of the Light Brigade*, metrically recounted from the point of view of a Russian gun-crew laughing fit to bust, on the ground, that poetry was not my bag – when a little lightbulb suddenly appeared in a bubble above my head, to be replaced an instant later by the dustjacket of *Snow White and the Seven Winners For Whom Stature Is No Impediment*. Not the catchiest of titles perhaps, but if you're looking for mega-sales nothing beats a book that does what it says on the tin, and here we have a community of dedicated but impoverished titchy mineworkers, living, through no fault of their own, a celibate life in a hole in the ground, who suddenly stumble upon a terrific-looking brunette, take her back to their pitiful premises, show her more caring concern than she would ever get from men twice their height, but – shrewdly thinking ahead – never lay a finger on her. And what is their reward for this impressive combination of kindness and restraint? She takes off with the first tall handsome horse-borne toff who catches her eye. Do the little guys take this lying down (admittedly not perceptibly different from their taking it standing up)? Not this time around, because they have figured it all out first. They have observed the loving couple for some time, disguised as shrubs (a boon of smallness), and they have photographs, they have tapes, they have tabloid contacts, they are sitting, wise to the irony, on a goldmine. They get to be as rich as Bernie Ecclestone or Paul Daniels. They live happily ever after.

Should I start typing it right now? Possibly, if I can just get this idea for a smash-hit play out of my head. I once saw something called I think, *Rosencrantz and Guildenstern are Dead*. Might have been *Deaf*, but anyway, they were these two assassins, and I thought at the time how much better it would have been if the play had focused on their victim instead; so I might well take a crack at that first. Am I spoilt for choice, or what?

Sticky Problem

For me, along with seven heart-broken per cent of my hapless countrymen, Monday was a really bad day. It was the day on which Consignia trashed all our dreams.

We had, of course, begun to fear that something of the sort would happen from the moment, a month or so back, when the coup was announced, the tacky new flag was run up over the post office, and the brutal dictatorship of Consignia declared its summary emergence into the startled community of nations: although we had no clear idea of either where Consignia presently stood, or where its territorial ambitions might begin or end, it wasn't hard to guess, from its very name, the sort of country with which the world would henceforth have, willy-nilly, to deal – a barren, sunless place, ruled by a tinpot dictator in elevated heels and waxed moustaches and a shimmering white uniform hung with big floppy epaulettes and self-appointed medals, where the native Consignian language derived from Old High Gobblede-gook and the people never smiled.

Oh, sure, you knew that if you were to ring them up they would say – after you had been forced to listen to a blaring hour or so of martial Muzak – welcome to Consignia, Craig speaking, how may I help you, but you would know that, behind his big steel desk, beneath the retouched aquatint of the generalissimo, Craig's ferret eyes were dead. So, sensing all this, 60 million Britons waited, biting their knuckles, for Consignia's first move.

It came in a press announcement on Monday morning. From that day forth, Consignia, which had somehow managed to seize sole and absolute control over all sticky pictures of our beloved Queen, would be selling those pictures in self-adhesive form, on rolls, in books, "in accordance with the wishes of 93 per cent of the British public". Our blood ran cold: was this extraordinary statistic mere propaganda, or was it true? I rang a few people I knew I could trust as belonging to the dissident seven per cent (if that was indeed how pitifully few we were) but this was the first that they, too, had heard of Consignia's poll: neither had they been approached for their opinion as to whether they preferred to lick or pluck,

53

nor did they know of anyone who had. Several voices trembled uncontrollably in my receiver: they had read on into the announcement and wanted to know what "state-of-the-art stamp-manufacturing technology" meant, or what "elimination of error and waste" indicated, or what "other gateway initiatives" might herald, but I could not answer. Who knew where this might end? Where it had begun was horrible enough.

For, even if this is not a *fait accompli* foisted upon the nation by bogus research – even if, that is to say, 93 per cent of my readers really were personally canvassed for their stamping of choice – I can only assume that their minds were elsewhere when they placed their ticks in the box provided. True, there will always be some eager to vote for anything that looks like progress, who will dismiss me as a Luddite, or a freak who gets off on the taste of gum, or a miser prepared to steam his fingers into saveloys for the pitiable reward of an unfranked 20p, or a sad old housebound jerk with so much time on his hands that he relishes the tiny jigsaws offered when a stamp is pulled ineptly from its sheet, leaving a little bit behind, Her Majesty's gracious ear, perhaps, which then has to be painstakingly slid and prodded, seamlessly, into place. But none of this is what I am on about.

I am on about the dreams adumbrated in my opening paragraph.

Because the last thing we seven per cent want is state-of-the-art stamp technology and the elimination of error: state-of-the-artless technology that leads to errant stamps is such stuff as dreams are made on. Unique among valuable artefacts, postage stamps depend for their often immense worth on the pure accident of somebody's ineptitude:

bidders do not engage in punch-ups in Sotheby's aisles if a Sèvres milkmaid with three ears comes up for auction, thieves do not abseil into the Rijksmuseum looking for a portrait Rembrandt punched his drunken fist through, but if a scanner goes on the fritz and a sheet of first-class orange comes out tartan, or a bloke suddenly stops his serrating machine to put the kettle on and the result is a row of stamps with perforations not down the edges but down the middle, the result may well be priceless.

And that is why seven per cent of us hurtle downstairs each morning at the letterbox's clunk, because you never know your luck.

Or at least, you never did. But, thanks to the grim initiators goose-stepping in unstoppable phalanx through the gateways of Consignia, you do now.

Domestic Drama

IN common with all who figured (or rather, didn't) in last week's news about plummeting audiences, I don't go to the theatre much, these days. I cannot handle it as once I could. Theatre drains me, now. Theatregoers will maintain that that is precisely what it is supposed to do, it is why man first put on a crude bark mask, painted his feet blue, and began hitting himself on the head with a pig's bladder to the atonal accompaniment of a three-holed bullrush; and I have no argument with that. It is simply that, as I grow older, I find that the emotional sturdiness of my earlier years daily grows feebler. An evening of theatre leaves me wrecked.

Especially when it is a long evening of theatre, like the one I recently experienced. Major, in every sense: an eight-hour performance of such extraordinary dramatic breadth, variety, and intensity that the dreamt recollection of it, several days on, can still hinge me upright on my midnight mattress, sweating and jabbering.

The performance began at 6pm, with a bourgeois *bonne-bouche* of an opening scene that had a touch of Coward about it, a smidgeon of Rattigan, a whiff of Ayckbourn. Set in a London bedroom, it features a woman who cannot find her other earring and a man who cannot find his other cufflink shouting increasingly barbed questions at one another about state of clothes, choice of restaurant, means of transport, location of tickets, future of marriage, and so on. They are about to phone lawyers when the doorbell rings. It is an Estonian asylum-seeker with a clapped-out Vauxhall, saying he was booked to take them to the Garlic Theatre in Leicester, he has looked in map, is long way, everyone must go quick quick. The husband explains, not without hand signals, about the Garrick Theatre off Leicester Square and the Estonian trudges off to sit in the Vauxhall for an hour, swearing. The next scene, which owes much to Beckett, is set in what seems to be a skip. It is in fact a Vauxhall, stuck in a contraflow outside Lewisham. The three occupants are screaming at one another. None of them knows why they are outside Lewisham. After a while, an old man bearing an uncanny resemblance to

56

Harold Pinter punches out the windscreen, pokes his head through, and gives them complex instructions about how to get from Lewisham to Leicester Square

Act II opens in the foyer of the Garrick Theatre, half an hour after the opening of *Feelgood*, with the couple trying to discover the secret of why people take £32 a seat off you and will not allow you to take the seat itself just because you have been in Lewisham, stuck in a play that has been going on while the play you have come to see has already started. The answer seems to be that Tom Stoppard has a lot to answer for, although there is some question about whether the question was Michael Frayn's. The husband goes to the stalls bar at this point and shouts at a lot of staff who aren't there. Eventually someone turns up and sells him two large whiskies for a sum which would have allowed him, in the days when he started going to the theatre, to buy his own pub.

We next see the couple (in an engaging little *trompe de théâtre* which invites comparison with Jean Cocteau) passing from the stage of their play into the auditorium to watch *Feelgood*, a piece in which a lot of actors shout at one another to scant purpose, as far as the husband can see an hour later, when he re-emerges into the foyer, carrying his wife, who always falls asleep. Both are starving, but (qv. Act I) neither has booked anywhere, because each had, of course, assumed that the other had done it. The wife says never mind, The Ivy is just around the corner.

Act III opens outside The Ivy. It might have opened inside, but for the fact that the next free table is on 3 March 2004, provided there is a cancellation. Since they cannot wait that long, the couple spend the next hour wandering through theatreland in a scene offering more than a passing nod to Edward Bond, looking no longer for a restaurant but for an all-night chemist to deal with the sprain of the husband's ankle caused by being shoved off the pavement by a mob of several hundred theatregoers with tattoos and stapled noses. Eventually they find a chemist, but it is so full of theatregoers waiting for midnight to transform their prescriptions into something to stuff into their stapled noses that the couple decide to hail a cab home.

But there is, of course, nothing to hail; so, poignantly redolent both of *Father Courage and his Swollen Bloody Ankle* and *Long Day's Journey Into North West London*, the play ends with the couple limping home at 2am to wonder aloud whether they should go to the theatre much, these days.

Woolly Thinking

CANNILY spotting, after only an hour or so in office, that there was not nearly enough to worry about these days, our feisty new Home Secretary has set out to strike terror into the hearts of a whole fresh catchment which hitherto thought itself safe. They are people who had always smugly believed themselves to be beyond the law of nature itself. They thought the very elements could not touch them. But they were wrong: for Mr

Blunkett is introducing legislation empowering coppers to snatch off balaclavas.

Now, I don't know what he does to the terrorists, the anarchists, the bank-robbers and anyone else wishing, not unreasonably, to conceal his identity from CCTV, but by God he frightens me. For I have worn balaclavas, man and boy, since the famously gelid winter of 1947, when I turned up in the Osidge Primary playground to find it occupied by what appeared to be a midget Norman army. I could, however, see them with only one eye: my mother being as maladroit a knitter as you could shake a needle at, not only were the eye-holes set so far apart that my ear poked out of the larger of them, but the wonky slit for my mouth was so much on the other side of my head that if I wanted to talk, I had to tug my balaclava round until I couldn't see anything at all. Indeed, when, that very same term, 36 of us sat chanting *The Charge of the Light Brigade*, it occurred to me that the blame for the otherwise inexplicable cock-up of Balaclava might well lie at the door of 600 mothers no less inept than mine, leaving their hapless sons to charge into the Valley of Death not only unable to see where they were charging, but also unable to ask the reason why. Either that, or Lord Cardigan's old mum was an equally rotten knitter who hadn't put the sleeves in the right place in his eponymous woollie, so that, though leading from the front, he was utterly stymied when it came to giving hand-signals.

But all that was long ago and faraway. I have a proper balaclava now, and when the mercury dives and the east wind strops its whetstone, there is no finer helpmeet to those wishing to hang on to noses and ears. But what shall comfort me once Blunkett's Bill has oiled its way into the statute book? Dare I chance a stroll across the frosty park, with dogs like PC Fang and Sergeant Radar panting in the shrubbery, waiting for the handler's nod? Dare I pop into my local bank some chilly morning, when I might alert the cornice lens to call down armed response units, which, expertly trained as they are to riddle anyone waving a cigarette lighter, would surely not shrink from emptying a Heckler & Koch at an ambiguous hat? Dare I even take my balaclava to the cleaners, or attempt to replace it when its day is done, knowing that beneath the counter there will almost certainly be a hidden button, wired in by Group 4 or some such reliable guardian of our liberties, to be pressed whenever a suspect comes in and begins asking questions about woollie headgear, so that helicopters may be speedily wheeled out and abseilers flak-jacketed?

My sole hope of continuingly snug winters lies in the possible backlash. For mark my words, Mr Blunkett, once the Old Bill starts whipping off balaclavas, brutally exposing young and old alike to runny noses, frostbitten extremities, chesty coughs and chapped lips, the Home Office will be up to its neck in civil actions before you can say Jack Frost. GPs will shut up shop at the sight of waiting-rooms teeming like Bhowani Junction. Entrepreneurs and unions will march together to condemn the terminal loss of sales and jobs when balaclavas are no more.

Police forces throughout the queendom will face long, expensive inquiries investigating institutional hattism, officers brutally shouted at by wheezy old ladies waving doctors' certificates will spend years in costly counselling before suing the Home Office for every penny it's got, and God alone knows what the outcome might be if a short-sighted copper were to spot the eyes and teeth of a black bloke in the foggy gloom of a December night and attempt to pull off his balaclava, only to discover that he wasn't wearing one. But even if all this fails, I have one last shot in my desperate locker; and, as so often in our communal past, it can be fired only by you, my beloved readers. I want each and every one of you, between now and winter, to buy (or knit) a balaclava and, at the first cold snap, pull it on and proudly walk abroad, so that every street and park and school and stadium and shopping centre and railway station billows with a rolling sea of wool.

And should any copper even dare to approach one of you, I want all the rest of you to throw up an arm and cry, with one bellowing voice: "I am Spartacus!"

Four Bad Legs

How infuriating that, yet again, Crufts based its judgments for this year's show on a farrago of entirely unreal qualifications for championship status, to a fanfare of mushy journalese. Why, I'll just bet that millions of dog-lovers have never even heard of the many richly deserved awards given each year for the REAL qualities of Britain's canine population. Isn't it time that they, too, came in for just a little press coverage?

☐ **The Gravy Dish:** The solid sterling silver Gravy Dish, presented annually at Panelbeaters Hall in the City, goes to the dog causing the most profitable tally of road accidents, and this year's runaway winner is the loveable border collie, Deaf. Although Deaf spent the latter part of the award year on only three legs, he still managed to cause 27 major road accidents at a total repair cost of more than £133,000, his *pièce de résistance* being a five-car pile-up involving a Ferrari Testarossa, a 1904 Rolls-Royce Silver Ghost, a milk-float, an 18-tonne Foden artic, a Metropolitan Police Range Rover, and a lollipop man. Well done, Deaf! The Special Mention Pour La Mérite collar-charm for Best Single Shunt went to Oscar, a chihuahua who sprang from his owner's cleavage on the M4 and bit her on the ear, causing her to drive her new Mercedes 500 SEL into an emergency phone-post, at a cost of £7,357, plus VAT.

☐ **The Dead Whale Prize for Industry:** For the second year running, the coveted award presented by the Sod-The-Whale Campaign on behalf of the British petfood industry has been won by Juliet Provo III, the Irish wolf-hound who, between April 2000 and April 2001, consumed 2.8 whalesworth of tinned food, 169.4 kilos of horse'n'donkey mince, and an unspecified amount of other processed materials about which the manufacturers were somewhat vague, although they were prepared to concede that wolfhound could not entirely be ruled out. Not, the chairman hastened to add, that there was the slightest need for embarrassment on that score: recycling was not only a highly commendable industrial process but also traditional, if he might remind dog-lovers of the famous case of Greyfriars Norman, the 19th-century fox terrier who has been eaten some 250 times, in various forms, since before the death of General Gordon.

☐ **The Golden Bootscraper:** Always hotly contested, this year's Golden Bootscraper, sponsored by the Doormats 'R'Us chain, went to Spot of Camden Town, a mongrel who, though completely untrained, not only succeeded in making almost two-thirds of Primrose Hill unfit for human use but also wiped out four beds of Ena Harkness in the Regent's Park Rose Garden, fused 11 Camden street-lamps, and was responsible for having a Baker Street phone-box melted down for scrap. Spot, already the winner of two Silver Bootscrapers, is said to be so excited at his latest success that he cannot contain himself.

☐ **The Quis Custodiet Award for Security Work:** This year's Quis Custodiet Brass Fang has been awarded posthumously to Mad Bloody Bastard IV of Securihound, a thoroughbred pit bull doberdingo who was guarding the premises of The Nearly New Mobile Telephone and VCR Company in Hackney when he noticed a group of kiddies playing football in the road outside. Though trained only to take the throat out of VAT inspectors, the dog nevertheless managed to bite his way through the chain-link fence and maul six of the children before tragically getting the worst of a courageous assault on a 137 bus.

☐ **The Man's Best Friend Miracle Offer Award:** This important prize, funded annually by The Guild of Advertising Copywriters Tuscan Farmhouse and Learjet Committee, goes each year to the dog most prepared to degrade itself in the effort to sell something nobody knew they wanted. This year, it has been won by Gustav Holst of Khazitex III, a yellow labrador who ran non-stop from Land's End to John o'Groat's, paying out a 600-mile roll of avocado-tinted mango-scented lavatory paper as he ran and managing to entangle such famous national landmarks as Nelson's Column, the late Wembley Stadium, York Minster, Ben Nevis, and Anne Robinson.

Particular honourable mention has been made of the fact that the dog, despite suffering the most alarming side-effects of his arduous run, did not even pause for breath at John o'Groat's but immediately picked up a second roll of Khazitex and ran back to Land's End, this time as a dachshund.

Royal Progress

THERE was, of course, boundless excitement among royal-watchers at Monday's momentous news that the Prince of Wales and Mrs Parker Bowles had, for the very first time, attended a church service together, in public. Now, while it is true that the church in question was on the Queen's Sandringham estate and therefore just a mite less public than we should, perhaps, have preferred – if I may put this in a context you can all comprehend, it was rather as if I and the future Mrs

Coren, a few patient years after having been introduced, had at last been seen standing in the garden shed on my old man's Kilburn estate at the same time – it is unquestionably a big leap forward.

It would, mind, have been even bigger had the couple walked in side by side; but discreet gradualism remaining, as ever, the tactic of choice, the Prince walked in with ex-King Constantine and ex-Queen Ann Marie of Greece – something I fear I am unable to put in a context you can all comprehend, since you could not get this many people into my old man's garden shed, certainly not without taking the mower out first – and Mrs Parker Bowles followed them in; later, but (it was stressed) through the same door. It was therefore no surprise that Monday's newspapers should have been so gobsmacked by this major breakthrough in what was described as "the normalisation of the relationship" – especially since it represented an exponential advance on their only previous joint public worship, in St John's Wood Synagogue in 1999, at the wedding of Miss Santa Palmer-Tomkinson and Mr Simon Sebag-Montefiore; for on that occasion, though the Prince wore a little hat and Mrs Parker Bowles a big one, just like any other shul-going couple – more or less – they had not only walked in separately, they had walked in through separate doors.

So things have come a long way, in just two years.

Which can lead only to rapt supposition about the future: what, in their gentle progress towards public normalisation, will the glittering couple be most likely to walk into next? My own guess is Tesco's, partly because more people go to Tesco's than to church and the act would thus gain the couple both wider public and more nondenominational endorsement, and partly because at Tesco's the double doors open automatically, avoiding tricky protocols about who went in first and through which one. In the twinkling of an eye, they would have gone in – without anybody taking offence at the impropriety – together. This could well happen as early as 2003, though they would, of course, have to push separate trolleys: I cannot, with the best will in the world, see them sharing a trolley until the winter of 2004, probably in time for their big Christmas shop; even then, it will still be too early for the Prince and Mrs Parker Bowles to have a public row about which aisle to steer towards – sprouts or Tia Maria – after they have selected the turkey. Nor, sadly, will the turkey selection have been allowed to spark the incandescent fury possible between a man who refuses to eat any poultry that has not been brought up in its own bungalow listening to Mozart and a woman who doesn't give a toss. Personally, I should love to see their relationship this normalised, since neither of them is getting any younger, but I appreciate that that is too much to expect, and it could well be as late as 2006 before they are screaming at one another in the car park about who left the bloody Volvo where; and as for one of them chucking the map out of the window as the other one makes his circuitous way towards his parents' place on Christmas morning, the apogee of normalisation, I think most authorities would agree that we're probably looking at 2008 or 09.

Could be even longer, mind, if Charles and Camilla are not in the same car at all, as the result of still not living in the same house at all: at the time of going to press, as far as the public record is concerned, these are two people who have spent the past quarter of a century occasionally bumping into one another, usually in the presence of vicars, rabbis or horses, and then separating again through different exits. God knows where they sleep.

So there you have the crux, possibly the rub – maybe even both, because that is just how crucially rubby it is: despite the truly astonishingly incredible exponential advance at Sandringham last weekend, how can the relationship between the Prince of Wales and Mrs Parker Bowles ever be normalised in the eyes of the great British public unless and until one of them is spotted letting the cat out, and, ten hours later, the other one is spotted letting it back in?

Through the same door.

Full Throttle

THERE's a special providence in the fall of a sparrow, observed the most major of Elizabethan hacks; and, as always, he was bang on the money, leaving the most minor of Elizabethan hacks able to offer nothing better by way of starters than a deferential tweak to his immemorial line. For there's a special providence in the fall of a pheasant, too: I observed this on Saturday when, coming upon a car-struck pheasant, my Elizabeth proved no whit less formidable than Shakespeare's by demonstrating that, though she has the body of a weak and feeble woman, she has the thumb and forefinger of a master strangler.

What, then, was so specially provident for me about that moment when Her Majesty was graciously pleased to throttle the dented bird? It was because the moment suddenly resolved an issue with which I, in common with millions of other concerned subjects, had been grappling for most of my life: she showed why we needed a monarchy. In snapping that stricken neck, she did what no president could have done, no prime minister, no elected panjandrum of any kind: for she fulfilled to the letter Napoleon's ringing dictum that true leadership is action without fear of consequences.

Imagine – and I wouldn't dream of asking you to if I thought you wouldn't enjoy it – Mr Blair in this same situation. Or, rather, similar situation, since neither of us, I'm sure, can begin to imagine the People's Poppet striding eagerly out in plus-twos and ear-muffs to fill the Norfolk welkin with pellets and plummeting dinners; let us instead imagine him snug and safely belted in the back of his Jaguar, being whisked to some assiduously threat-proofed rural moot to deliver to an adoring claque a length of innocuous pabulum by divers hands. Suddenly, there is a soft bonk, the sort of noise you get when windscreen meets feather; the car slews to a halt, as do the cars fore and aft, and the lane fills with marksmen assuming the position.

But there is no rattle of terrorist ordnance from the hedges, there are no grenades hurtling from haystacks, there are no unauthorised helicopter gunships, there is no sound at all except a faint pitter-patter of wings flapping on tarmac. The minders seek the source, and spot it, and raise a reassuring thumb to the Prime Minister's driver. The Prime Minister now alights, peers, and asks what it is. A minder tucks his gun away and, taking *The Special Branch Book of Birds* from his other holster, replies, after a bit, that it is a pheasant. More than that – and here he nudges it with his toe – it is a damaged pheasant.

Everybody now looks at their leader, since the situation clearly requires a response of some kind, but which? There could be mileage in this, there could be a percentage, but then again there could also be a downside. The PM is minded to bind up the pheasant's wounds, sit it on his knee, and arrive at their destination cradling it in his arms, for there is a full two hours before the *Six O'Clock News*. Mr Alastair Campbell, on the other hand, is for treading on it, because that would show a lack of squeamishness on the PM's part, you never know when you might be called upon to flatten Kosovo again, sunshine, but the PM is concerned that it might upset animal rights activists if he appeared on the news with a beak on his shoe.

It is at this point that the PM's PPS, Mr Bruce Grocott, coughs discreetly and says that it would hugely improve Mr Blair's standing with the Countryside Alliance if he wrung the bird's neck, it would show that he wasn't just some urban tosser, pardon his French, but the Prime Minister turns slightly green at this and has to lean against the car for a bit, so the Special Branch man says, please, sir, can we shoot it, sir, they do not let us shoot living things up Aldershot, it is all cardboard nig-nogs on pulleys etcetera, it would cheer the squad up no end if we could give it a proper seeing-to, but this does not go down at all well with Mrs Blair QC, who detaches little Leo from his lunch, adjusts her clothing, and, through her window, recites 14 different laws concerning the unwarranted discharge of firearms, and for God's sake start smiling again, people are driving past, they have camcorders, they have votes.

So Mr Blair asks Mr Campbell if he should phone Bill Clinton, he would know what to do, wouldn't he, he always does, and Mr Campbell says too bloody right, he would give it the kiss of life, probably just for starters, and how would that play when it's leaked to the *Guardian*, let's get the hell out of here, and they do, and the deserted pheasant goes flap-flap-flap ever more slowly, until it expires, because, as a special providence reminded me last Saturday, the truth is that, in a great democracy, only the unelected can make snap decisions.

Concrete Jungle

I SHALL not visit this year's Chelsea Flower Show. It is exhibiting a Help the Aged garden. The garden would not help this Aged: it would make this Aged shout and weep with rage, and you do not want to do that in public, if you are an Aged. It might attract a St John Ambulance brigadier, who would sit you down and loosen your collar and caringly inquire whether you had remembered to take your medication that morning; and if you explained that you were shouting and weeping with rage because there was a garage beside the Help the Aged garden with a car in it, that would only make matters worse. You could end up in a St John's funny farm

A photograph of the exhibit was in Monday's newspapers. It is a 1960s suburban front garden, designed, literally, to summon up nostalgia. It did that, all right: it summoned up nostalgia for the days when suburban houses had cars in garages beside them. Before, that is to say, they had cars in gardens in front of them, and when I tell you that that is one of the main reasons I moved out of Cricklewood, you, more than most, will perhaps understand about the shouting and the weeping. For when I moved into Cricklewood, at the end of that self-same decade, the lucky rambler could stroll the tree-lined suburban streets and rejoice at the horticultural plethora that hit his every sense at every level: lilac, magnolia, bay and eucalyptus bent to the vernal breeze above his head, exhaling their myriad perfumes and perched with choralling birds; yew and privet and broom and berries took the hedgy eye-line just beneath, and every few yards that line was broken and gloriously illuminated by the floribundal glimpses down countless garden paths, paved crazily between a dozen rhododendrons, a hundred roses, a thousand dahlias, and of course, a million silver bells and cockle shells, and pretty maids all in a row. Because that was how our gardens grew, then; indeed, our very houses seemed to grow, their mundane brick and tile and stucco delightfully embroidered with clutching honeysuckle and wistaria and japonica and clematis, as each suburbanite, even as he trained the roses

71

round his door, pursued his dream of subrurality. Hooked since earliest infancy on the irresistible propaganda of pastoral jigsaws, the mighty mass of Greater Londoners combined to fit their assorted suburbs together into the biggest pastoral jigsaw of them all. And more yet than this, it smelt and sounded as mere coloured cardboard cannot do, because the trees and shrubs and borders, the tubs and trellises and pots, were filled not only with umpteen different scents but with umpteen different birds and bugs – a unique suburban ecology in a self-contained sub-rural world, like nothing that there had ever been before.

But heartbreakingly, it is no longer. For do you know what grows in those same front gardens, now? Volvos and Alfas and Jags and Datsuns, and four-wheel-drives all in a row. They do not grow on grass, of course, because the lawns have all been ripped up, they grow on ochre precast cobblettes and ersatz Yorkstone slabs and magenta chip-stuck asphalt and herringbone terracotta tiles, behind, not high green English hedges, but low grey Dutch walls, with reproduction Victorian lamp-posts at their corners. Nor are they to be found under blossoming trees, because trees mean birds, and birds mean droppings on the shimmering cellulose. The perfumes they give off are Shell and Dunlop and Simoniz, and their colours are electric blue, metallic scarlet, chrome. Their sap and nectar drip from sump and crank-case, and the only insects they attract are the sad flat corpses stuck to grille and headlamp – briefly, mind, until the dedicated gardener in his spotless Gucci wellies hurtles out to hose them off, because that is what watering is all about, these days.

So they're clearly somewhat different now, suburban dreams. People, it seems, no longer want to sit in front of bay windows, gazing out contentedly at what they've grown, they want to sit there gazing out contentedly at what they've acquired, fantasising, perhaps, about an unfettered Charlie Dimmock jogging round to lean over the bonnet and give it a vigorous waxing, but above all thinking: "We are cool, we have made it, we do not have cheesy front gardens, we have swish carriage drives, we are townsfolk, we are not sub anything, we are super everything, we inhabit Greater Central London, we live on the inskirts!"

Well all right, fine, do what you like, sod the Aged, but tell me how the Royal Horticultural Society is going to summon up suburban nostalgia 40 years from now? Put on the Chelsea Motor Show?

Dead Beat

CONCERNED citizens will, I know, have been as thrilled as I to learn that the Home Office is to boost police ranks by encouraging elderly constables – resonantly described as "PC Dixons" – to stay on after retirement age. I, of course, wasted no time in speeding round to Dock Green nick to find out when the scheme was to begin, only to discover it to be already under way: for, as I walked in, a figure yet older and portlier than I glanced up from the whistle he was polishing to a spotless glint, saluted, and before I could even open my mouth, boomed:

"Evening all! Well, that about winds up another successful week here at the Green. You'll be glad to know we got a result in the case of the darkie I approached on suspicion last Monday, who, when asked: 'What are you up to, Sambo, loitering only half a mile from Ratner's, purveyors of fine jewellery to the carriage trade?' gave a reply I could not repeat to a gent like you, inviting a clip round the ear in which I was happy to oblige him, only to lose several teeth in the ensuing scuffle. Luckily, these were later found and turned in, and are now, after a dunking in hot Steradent, as good as new. As for chummy, he had it away on his toes and I was unable to catch him, due partly to the fact that these people can't half run, and partly to my truss-buckle coming undone in the fracas, but it is only a matter of time before the long arm of the law collars him, or someone similar.

"I was also instrumental in sorting out a domestic, the day after. I was proceeding up Mafeking Terrace when a lady run out and said the bloke next door was knocking his missus about. Despite my sciatica playing up again, I effected entry to the premises with my boot, and, discovering a woman with a black eye, told her to shut up so her husband could explain what was going on. He said he had come home to find no hot dinner on the table. I asked her if this was true, and, if so, what she had to say for herself. Failing to receive a satisfactory answer, I took her old man on one side and read him his rights, eg, three cooked meals a day, slippers ready on doormat, bins taken out, regular seeing-to of a Saturday night, and so forth, which, if explained in words of one syllable to his wife, should avoid the need to stick one on her. Another case all wrapped up, thanks to compassionate policing.

"Bit of a setback on Wednesday, mind. I got a shout to a burglary, suspect still on premises, but when I arrived, the kettle was definitely not on. I told the householder that it was official procedure to give an investigating officer a steaming hot cuppa – milky, four lumps, plus Garibaldi biscuit or Hob Nob as available – before he opened his notebook, you cannot lick a pencil with a dry wossname, but as I was informing him of this, the suspect belted out through the front door and jumped on to my bike, which I had left leaning against the wall, rather than chain to the gate, due to the combination having six digits, requiring a superhuman feat of, what's the word, memory, never mind having to bend down to undo it, you might not straighten up again – which is also why I have given up flexing my knees when going 'Allo, allo, allo.' Still, I had the last laugh, as the law always will: it is a major offence nicking police vehicles, and once I had polished my specs I was able to spot him passing a bus and thus identify him as almost certainly a man, more than likely in a hat. The bus was either a Number 11 or a Number 77, or just possibly a 17 or a 71, and once CID track down everyone on it and find out what they witnessed, it will be only a matter of time before I get my old Rudge back and the culprit is accidentally falling down Dock Green staircase.

"But this job is not all dedicated policework and ensuring deaf-aid batteries in working order at all times: you occasionally need a bit of luck, and I cannot give you a better for instance than the events of this very morning.

75

I clocked this bloke talking to himself in the High Street, probably an escaped loony with any number of Her Majesty's gracious bins on the lookout for him, but when I went up to him he gave me a load of old tosh about being on the blower. Well, any fool could see the thing he was waving at me didn't have a dial or a cord or anything, but this was not enough to arrest him on suspicion of being off his head. It was then that Lady Luck stepped in: as he took the thing away from his ear, I saw he was wearing an earring! Now, I can tell you are a man of the world, sir, I know I do not have to draw pictures, he was obviously about to make me a lewd offer such as the one I have just jotted in my notebook, am I right? If you want a butcher's at him, by the way, try the peep-hole in cell Number 4.

"But mind how you go."

Short Arm of the Law

As if to prove that it is never too late for anything, I seem, in this September song of hackery, to be turning into a crime correspondent. It is a role I have always rather fancied: the battered fedora, the ragged cheroot poking unlit through the five o'clock shadow, the baggy trenchcoat, the titchy camera, the dented hip-flask, the world-weary eye, the red-spotted bandanna caringly mopping the cheeks of the weeping moll with the fist-smeared lipstick and the terrific legs even as the Woodbined finger presses the button on the rib-taped recorder – I am, as we hard men say, well up for all that.

So welcome to part two of my noviciate as relentless scourge of Yard and Home Office alike. A few pages back, I brought you an exclusive interview with one of the clapped-out PC Dixons whom David Blunkett is trying to woo back into service, and today I address yet another of his truly inspired force-bolstering initiatives: the plan for certain police duties and powers to be assigned to a "middle tier of uniformed civilians consisting of traffic wardens and other trained community officials, all deploying their particular expertise". Now you, when you saw this leaked report in your newspapers, may well have applauded the notion of a para-copper force of traffic wardens taking on major blaggers and getting seven bells knocked out of them, but you may also have wondered how that particular expertise of theirs would work in practice. What, in short, will traffic wardens be empowered to do?

So, once more, I have pursued my investigations on your behalf, contacting a well-known metric grass whom, to protect her identity, I shall call Deep Rita. And here is what I have gleaned of Mr Blunkett's hitherto secret proposals: though meter attendants will not be allowed to arrest anyone directly, should they spot anyone acting suspiciously they will be empowered to issue them with a ticket and tape it to their chest, requiring them to report to a police station. It will be an offence to say the ticket blew off in the wind. If a serious crime is believed to have taken place, the meterperson may call up the assistance of a colleague and clamp the suspect, to await police. Should the police be too busy, a trained and uniformed community official, could be a bus driver, could be a dustman, will collect the suspect and remove him to a villain pound, to await police collection. Unless through computer error, he will not be crushed. At my canny probing, Deep Rita agreed that these procedures did involve risk of assault on meter-persons, but disclosed that since Mr Blunkett would anticipate this by making it a custodial offence even to give a meter attendant a funny look, she felt safe enough.

Although she could not say the same for the Lollipop Force. This, a source close to Mr Blunkett had told her up Tesco's, would be auxiliary to the Meter Branch, empowered not only to free up meterpersons for police duty by taking over the issuing of tickets and clamps as they made their way from one crossing to another, but also to man those crossings to assist the police directly. In the event, say, of a police flash to Lollipop Centre alerting a car chase, lollipersons would be deployed at zebras along the route to hold up their official signs, either slowing the villains to allow the police to catch up, or aggravating their offence to manslaughter, thereby getting them banged up for even longer. I asked Deep Rita if lollipersons had agreed to this major new role, and she told me that the vast majority had, since they were not only stone-deaf but looking the other way when the question was put.

But mightn't these new deployments create a serious lollipower shortage, as the attendants were rushed to emergency action? No problem, replied Deep Rita, Mr Blunkett was ahead of me there: she had seen page 398 of the report, where plans were set out for the manning of temporarily vacated pedestrian crossings by yet another section of the uniformed community. Which? I asked. Beefeaters, said Rita: not only do they stand out a treat, day or night, but they are well versed in the carrying of halberds. These will get a STOP sign gummed to them, and have the added advantage in the event of motorists not pulling up in good time or people on Zimmer frames taking all bloody day, of being able to administer a sharp poke beyond the capacity of a normal lollipop.

And was it her information, I inquired finally, that all these plans had been fully researched? No question, replied Rita, her hairdresser's uncle had been cleaning the Home Office windows at the time, and whenever a new proposal was outlined to Mr Blunkett's dog Lucy, she definitely barked twice for yes.

I Think It's All Over

THEY say bad things come in threes. I don't know who the they are who say this, mind, or how they found out that that was how bad things came, because I have never actually heard them walking around saying it, but I am here to confirm that, last weekend, they were spot on. Worse yet, the three bad things were all inter-connected, and, worst of all, they all carried me back to my sweet remembered yesteryear, and trod on it.

The first bad thing was Saturday's report that the German post office was celebrating this year's World Cup by issuing six commemorative stamps, each in honour of six previous winners, and each to be sold not only in Germany, but also in the country commemorated. The six previous winners are Brazil, Germany, Uruguay, Italy, Argentina, and France. Hang about, you murmur, wasn't there a seventh previous winner? You are not wrong. So where is its stamp? It is nowhere: Germany is not issuing anything to commemorate its being hammered into 1966 oblivion by England. Sour grapes? Sour krauts? Not so, they protest, it is solely because the English stamp would have to bear the head of the Queen, and this could not be incorporated into a soccer scene. Oh, really? Is there in all Germany not a single designer ingenious enough to depict, say, a Bobby Moore inch-perfect cross sailing into the goalmouth to meet our gracious sovereign's head rising above the stranded defenders and nodding a belter past Tikouski's helpless glove? Bordered, perhaps, by a titchy Gothic script recording: "Sie denken das alles über ist – es ist jetzt!" Apparently not. Instead, it is *Deutschland uber alles*. I cannot tell you how far that lowered me, on Saturday night.

Nor how far further I was lowered, on Sunday morning, by the news that Oxford's hospitals are working to only 40 per cent of their capacity because of a nurse shortage. What? A nurse *what*? A *what* shortage? Tell me the apes have quit Gibraltar, tell me the swallows have failed to come back to Capistrano, but do not tell me the nurses are fleeing Oxford. Nurses were the main reason that the men who were boys when I was a boy swotted their brains out to get into the place. Oxford boasted greater nurses than anywhere else in the academic world, there had been nurses at Oxford since 1252, stonemasons building Balliol would deliberately hammer their thumbs flat just to get near them, and of the clerical novices who, a few years later, became the first undergraduates, more than 80 per cent chucked in the devotional sponge in order to run off with girls in black stockings who had been called in to balance their humours.

Who is to blame for the current crisis? No, not the Department of Health this time, it is Education and Transport that are at the bottom of all this: in the days when students had all fees paid and generous grants, they could buy pre-MOT bangers for a tenner and still have enough left over to take a nurse out for a nice horse curry before driving her back to a hostel with unlocked sashes. And since the students then were not scuzzy unwheeled paupers reading for degrees in speed garage or the early years of Ali G and going on to a career selling *The Big Issue* in Kathmandu, but elegant men in cavalry twill and Chelsea boots and college ties studying stuff that would one day ensure £600 a year from Shell or the FO, Oxford's nurses could often be terminally cajoled by the possibility of a three-carat finger, a flash thrash at Caxton Hall and a bijou cottage in Cadogan Square.

Nor was any harm at all done when, in 1959, *Carry on Nurse* came out: my undergraduate generation was immediately driven even more nurse-nuts by the highly accessible subtext, which made anything state-registered a must-have accessory incalculably more desirable than a Blue, a First, or a toaster that actually popped up; and this was tickety-boo for Oxford's-nurses, because they didn't

81

all have to look like Shirley Eaton, they could look like Hattie Jacques and still not walk away empty-handed. And yes, I do know I shall get furious letters about this, but what the hell, feminist correctness has had a good run for its money; and because I have been so deeply jolted by the wheel's coming off Time's winged chariot, I have sort of ceased caring. I had a rotten Sunday, staring out into the sleet and wondering where the 43 years had gone since my best friend and I last drove a Morris Ten out to Boars Hill with six student midwives in the back.

The third bad thing? Ok, you asked for it, or one of us did, and it was the announcement of the annual change of items on the Retail Price Index. Tinned salmon, the *ne plus ultra* and *sine qua non* of my student tea-times, has been removed, because nobody eats it any more; and leg-waxing has been included. Suddenly, I feel very old, and very hairy.

Going by the Book

FAY Weldon's latest novel, *The Bulgari Connection*, earned her a fat fee from the eponymous Italian jewellers in return for building her plot around a Bulgari necklace. Now, while I have no problem with that, I am just a little uneasy that unscrupulous publishers might start tampering with bestselling texts on their backlists, in greedy expectation of a placement bob or two...

From *Rebecca*:

Last night I dreamt I went to Manderley again.

An imposing Gntlmns Estate, which wld suit Ambassador or smlr, it stnds in its own grnds of 36 ACRES, inclding rvr w. troutfshng, TWO pddcks, wide rnge of outbldngs, mature lndscped gdns of app. 3 ACRES with brd snny asp & 400yds drct frntge to FAMED BTY SPT, the Helford. The hse itslf has been CMPLTLY MDNISED, to inclde GAS ch & lg-fired sauna. Wealth of xposd bms, 10 beds, 6 bths, plus stff qurtrs (or grnny flt), 4 HUGE receps, bllrm, bllrd rm, gn rm, htd swmmng pl. SBSNTIAL OFFRS INVTD FOR F/HOLD. Contact Knight, Frank & Rutley, 20 Hanover Square, Wl.

Mrs Danvers was standing in the hall as I entered from the . . .

From *The First Book of Kings*:

1. Now king David was old and stricken in years; and they covered him with clothes, but he gat no heat.

2. Wherefore his servants said unto him, Let there be sought for my lord the king a young virgin: and let her stand before the king, and let her cherish him, that my lord the king may get heat.

3. But the king said unto them, Never mind virgins, what I am after is one of them Berry Magicoal items where it flickers just like a real fire only it is ten times as warm and also running on off-peak wossname; for it will keep me warm as toast and not dent my wallet, neither.

4. So they sought for such a fire, even unto their nearest stockist; and they took there the advantage of a miracle offer, which was an electric egg-timer with every fire purchased.

5. And when king David saw what they had brought with them, he waxed exceeding...

From *The Adventures of Sherlock Holmes*:

"Is there any other point to which you would wish to draw my attention?"

"To the curious incident of the dog in the night-time."

"The dog did nothing in the night-time."

"That was the curious incident," said Sherlock Holmes.

"I fail to see why that is curious."

"When a dog is fed on nourishing Kennomeat," said Holmes wearily, "it not only enjoys a rich glossy coat, it also does regular poo-poos."

"Excellent!" I cried.

"Elementary," said he.

From *A Farewell To Arms*:

Then the car was over the bridge and out of sight behind the trees. I waved to Aymo, and climbed down, and crouched beside the railway embankment. Aymo came down and squatted beside me.

"Did you see the car?" I asked.

"No. We were watching you."

"A pity," I said. "It had discs all round, electric windows, ABS, full air-conditioning, quad stereo."

"All as standard?" he said.

"Yes,' I said.

"Cojones," he said. "I am sorry I missed it."

"It is of no importance," I said. "You can see it at your nearest Skoda dealer. You can take it for a test-drive any time. It is what they do."

"Is it as good a car as they say?" he said.

"Yes," I said. "It is the best car there is."

From *Carry On Jeeves*:

There was another ring at the front door. Jeeves shimmered out and came back with a parcel from which the scarlet letters DHL shone forth like a good deed in a naughty world.

"Dashed efficient johnnies, DHL," I remarked, indicating the item under review, "unlike those feckless bloaters Consignia."

"And remarkably reasonable, sir," murmured Jeeves, with that what-is-it in the voice which I have noticed creeps into the glottal works of people when the talk turns to folding money. "I am given to understand that a quite substantial packet may be dispatched to Outer Mongolia for hardly more than the price of a pink gin."

"Not what one would call an easy decision, that," I remarked.

"I beg your pardon, sir?"

"Whether to contact one's Mongolian aunt or get outside a pink gin, Jeeves," I expatiated.

"Were the gin to be Gordon's, sir," replied Jeeves, "I am of the humble opinion that the lady in question would, as racing parlance has it, be left at the post."

Air Raid Warning

I HAVE a folded Put-U-Up in my shelter. It is not truly a Put-U-Up, mind, since U are not going to be put up on it; if anyone is going to be put up on it, I am. Along with Mrs Coren. Alongside Mrs Coren. The question is: when should I put it up, so that I can put us up on it? Because putting it up will demand a major decision. Putting it up will constitute a major act.

This question would never have been raised in Cricklewood, because in Cricklewood everything else was raised. If we had wanted to put U up in Cricklewood, up is where we should have put U, because up is where the Put-U-Up was. We did not have a down. Had anything happened in Cricklewood, we could not have sped down into the shelter in the hope of mitigating the happening, because we did not have a shelter. We should have had to remain on the ground floor, possibly under the dining-table, grinning and bearing it, since there was nothing below the ground floor. But that was long and far away – as my mother used to sing in the Last Lot – and when we moved here from Cricklewood, here had a shelter. We did not call it a shelter, then, of course: we called it a cellar. Even though the estate agent called it an as-yet unconverted sub-garden room with enormous potential. Unwitting foresight, eh? Did he see 9/11 coming? He would call it a cellar now, all right, and point out that its enormous potential was for sheltering, given that this might well add a bob or two to the asking price, in a falling market (if U wish at this point to make a weedy pun about a falling market, feel free, but please keep it to yourself: I have major decisions to make).

We did not, however, convert it, because we saw its enormous potential for getting filled with all the Cricklewood junk that Help the Aged wouldn't take, such as the Put-U-Up – a smart decision on their part, because if the aged ever wanted to put the Put-U-Up up, they would have needed a great deal of help. Never mind the fact that after it has been put up, it has a tendency to put itself down again: it could suddenly snap shut with something aged trapped inside it like a stranded turtle, waving its arms and legs about. That is why Mrs Coren and I will have to leap on it together, with great timing, so that our combined weight keeps it flat. But that is not what makes the decision, or the act, major. U know what is going to do that.

Being sub-garden, it is very like the Anderson shelter of my infancy. It was not built by Anderson, though, because it was built in 1826, by a man called Ambrose Poynter. It is a Poynter shelter. I cannot be certain why he built it, but my guess is that, although Napoleon, being dead, was no longer a threat to British security, his son and heir – as it were Napoleon bin Bonaparte – was still an unknown quantity, and the apple never falling far from the tree, Poynter thought a shelter might well add a bob or two to the asking price.

In any event – OK, in one event – what am I going to put in it, besides Mrs Coren? In the Last Lot, I can just about remember an earlier Mrs Coren carrying in a hundredweight of Spam and cocoa, and a wind-up gramophone to enable us to keep in constant communication with Vera Lynn. The Corens have gone up in the world a bit since then, but that serves only to make it harder to choose what in the world to take down: a hundredweight or two of *pâté de foie gras* and Chateau Petrus might be just the menu to put by for a rainy day, especially if the rain were a bit iffy, but a couple of weeks might well prove too much of a good thing; so, after spending an increasingly fraught hour with a notebook at Waitrose before going nuts, I trudged home and sought the advice of the later Mrs Coren. Who made the interesting observation that during the Last Lot, takeaway food had not yet been invented, but now we could simply put our trust in Domino's Pizza. When I asked her how we could be sure they would still be standing or that the kid on the bike would get through, she replied that there were so many branches that one of them was bound to survive, and that even if the kid had to bike from Cheltenham or Rhyl, he would get through, they always did, though she was prepared to concede that the anchovies might have begun to curl. Then she looked at me for a bit. I have come to know that look, down the long arches of the years.

Well, one of us will have to take me seriously, and once again it looks like being the one with a lifetime's training and experience in staring out of the loft window wondering if anything interesting is going to happen. So, on the off-chance that it might, I shall pop downstairs now, oil the hinges on the Put-U-Up, and test it out. Just by lying on it, of course: I wouldn't want to be caught napping.

To Boldly Go

Bᴀᴅ news. I have not heard from the Royal Geographical Society. Again. This makes 2002 the 36th consecutive year I have not heard from them. Since now is the season when the RGS contacts the fortunate dozens whose applications for expedition grants have found favour, I must assume, once more, that I am not of that number.

I know about that number: I have read every annual announcement, and bitten my envious lip at the academic minimalists who have gone off to record the flute music of the Chang-Pas nomads or clock the dirt cone behaviour on Cotopaxi or chart the growth rate of Arctic moss, and I have envisaged, each time, a tear falling from the niched statue in the RGS wall. It is David Livingstone's: can those who clutch the cashboxes behind that wall have so forgotten the momentous achievements of the inspired amateur? Has the RGS, in short, turned its back for ever on The Great Quest?

Since 1971, for example, I have been desperately attempting to interest it in funding my expedition to find

King Solomon's Skip. It is a well-known fact, for which a huge body of documentation exists, that anyone who keeps anything on the grounds that it will one day come in handy, eventually throws it out. The day after it is taken away, it comes in handy. Legend has it that all such items finally end up in a giant skip somewhere in Equatorial Africa. The skip was originally built by King Solomon, who – having 1,000 wives – spent his entire life asking what happened to his old mohair jacket, his set of tools with five drills missing, scroll two of *How To Cook*, his left tartan slipper, and so forth, as the result, naturally, of the old mohair trousers, the five drills, scrolls one and three, his right tartan slipper, and so forth, suddenly turning up at the back of the stair-cupboard.

There have been several reported sightings of the skip by natives, and one solid piece of evidence from no less luminary a figure than Mungo Park, who in 1797 saw two natives running along the opposite bank of the Niger with a lavatory he had thrown out of his house in Selkirk three years earlier.

I have been submitting my charts and costings for this major quest – including an offer to the RGS of 5 per cent of the take plus all the old mattresses they can carry – for 35 years, but these have been met with as little enthusiasm as my bid to discover The Car Park of Prester John. The outline for this, as any RGS pennypincher could testify, has been on my files since 1958, when England's first parking-meter was ceremonially topped out on the firm promise that all the money to be manufactured therefrom would go towards building municipal off-street parking lots which would make the Hanging Gardens of Babylon look like the Shankill Road. None of these has yet been sighted, but rumours persist that one was in fact built, 500ft tall, with individual carpeted lock-ups, Muzak-free lifts, a crèche, a Michelin-starred restaurant complex, wardens to ensure against dog suffocation, and a carjacker-proof electrified fence, the whole shebang open 24 hours a day, at no charge whatever.

All I need is two bearers and the occasional Dakota-drop. The RGS, however, preoccupied as it is with ringing jellyfish, tapping trees, counting pebbles and other such unimaginative exercises, will have none of it. Nor has one whit of interest been expressed in my mooted expedition to crack the mystery of The Consignia Triangle, that bizarre force-field into which all second-class mail disappears never to re-emerge, or even my search for El Dorado, which senior readers may recall was a major ice-cream that vanished around 1955, leaving mankind to get by on little tubs of lard ripple with a plastic cherry on.

Well, they have had their chance. After much patriotic heart-searching, I have decided to ignore the RGS altogether, just as it has chosen to ignore me. Next year, I intend to seek private sponsorship for my latest and greatest expedition. It will be an attempt to reach the West Pole, which, lying as it does in the middle of the Seychelles, calls for no huskies, sleds ponies, tractors, quilted freezewear, or expensive tins to keep toes in.

All I need is a litre of Ambre Solaire, a pair of Ray-Ban Wayfarers, a first-class seat on the aisle, and a Union Flag to claim the place for Her Gracious Majesty.

It may interest the RGS to learn how I shall raise the necessary funding. It is my intention to mount a preliminary foray to contact the elusive creature –

believed to be living high among the deep slush of the mighty Hindujas – known as the Sub-continental Abominable Conman. Abominable he may be, but when it comes to patronage, his generosity is the stuff of legend. Having done some preliminary research, I now intend to set up a rude hide as close to Downing Street as possible.

Backseat Driver

WATERLOO, please.

I realise it is the opposite direction, I realise it is almost certainly your turn-round time, you do call it turn-round time, I believe, yes I thought you called it turn-round time, I appreciate you will want to join your family in Crayford, am I right, just nod, I thought so, I am rarely wrong, you look an Essex type to me, you get to know these things as a passenger, I had a driver the other day, you won't believe this, I had a driver the other day, straight up, I had driver in the cab the other day, I said to him, don't tell me, Gant's Hill, you are definitely a resident of Gant's Hill, I thought he'd have a heart attack, I thought he'd have a heart attack right there at the wheel, well it wouldn't be the first time, did you realise there were 178 heart attacks in cabs in the metropolitan area alone last year?

Not a lot of people know that.

Yes, I realise, as I say, that it is your turn-round time, you will already be thinking of Crayford and your new snooker table, not full-size but then who has the space these days, still you can get just as good a game on a half-size especially with a slate-bed, it costs mind, what doesn't, but what I say is, we only pass this way but once, you're a long time dead, there are no 147 breaks in the cemetery, narmean? They say I'm a bit of a philosopher, well you have to be in this game, you have to be a bit of a philosopher as a passenger, you meet all sorts but you have to take them as you find them, drivers, don't get me going on drivers, still it wouldn't do if we were all made the same, if God had wanted us all the same he would've put chimney pots on our heads, catch my drift? Take that driver who came up before Mr Justice Wossname on Monday, I say Mr Justice, he was actually a Sir Sunnink, but even if they are sirs in real life they are misters when they are on the bench, did you know that, not that it is really a bench, of course, in the full meaning of the word, it is not a bench as you and I would recognise it, it does not have tools or sparrows on it, it is called a bench because it was originally an actual bench in 1321, I tell a lie, 1327, when the law all started, they did it in the open air, they put up this bench under a tree and the judge sat on it and judged people.

That was how wigs came about. Being under a tree, there was a risk of droppings, which could well have brought the law into disrespect: people up on a serious charge, the full solemnity of the law as the phrase is, and all of a sudden, splash, I trust I do not have to draw pictures, we are both men of the world, but they could not allow him to wear a hat due to holy oaths being taken, so what they did, they invented the wig. You wouldn't believe the state wigs got in, in the early days of the law. Until it came inside.

Where was I? Oh, yes, that judgment: this cab driver copped a hundred-quid fine for slagging off a fare who'd got out of his cab prior to agreed destination due to where he no longer wished to put up with said driver's rabbiting, I mean has the world gone mad, this is not what the courts are for, this is not why our forefathers sat under trees getting shat on, am I right? Next thing you know the Carriage Office'll be on your neck, hanging a black box round it to monitor your conversation, never mind pulling you in for not having a bale of hay on your roof, ha-ha-ha, they will be interviewing you on the accuracy of your statistics, eg, exactly how many illegal towel-heads flood here every day, stepping out without warning on our zebras, knocking our wing-mirrors off with their handlebars, and pushing up the price of diesel to pay for their herpes treatment? You might even be called upon to provide third-party corroboration of all the cross-dressing MPs who have thrown up on your back seat during the current parliamentary session.

No, you and I have knocked about a bit, we know there is only one way to deal with all this, and that is to slug it out word for word, man to man, and, here's a segue, an interesting spelling, I shall come back to that later – here's a segue, shall I tell you an interesting fact about homosexuals? In 1236, what is now Stuttgart was saved from total destruction when a gay wainwright gave the alarm after a fire broke out in a Job Centre. To this day, poofs can hold hands on the steps of the Rathaus without so much as a by-your-leave. A Rathaus is not a rat-house, of course, it is a, it is something else

94

entirely, did you know that? I don't know what the German is for rat-house, it is a pity I didn't ask the Jerry I had in the front of the cab in Dusseldorf the other day, he was amazed to learn that in 1945 you could have any woman in Berlin for a bar of fruit-and-nut – don't turn down here, it's twice as quick and half as expensive if you go up Whitefriars Street, am I right? Just nod.

Memory Lane

MY heart goes out, this morning, to the Pembrokeshire Coast National Park Authority; not something which regular readers might have been expecting my heart to do, perhaps, but that is only because regular readers may not know that, this morning, the Pembrokeshire Coast National Park Authority's own heart will, I hope, be going out to such a Stuttaford-alerting extent that it will need all the cardiac help it can get. For today is the day upon which the PCNPA council meets to vote on whether to stop allowing the benevolent bereaved to put up brass-plaqued seating in heartfelt memory of departed friends and relatives.

I sensed your own heart miss a beat, just then. It was no doubt stopping to wonder why, when 70 such memorial benches have been comfortingly dotted along the 186 miles of spectacular coastal path for many years, together with a further 25 commemorative bits and bobs, a vote should suddenly be taken to ban this generous and touching practice. Well, tell your heart this: ramblers have complained that the memorials are depressing. To quote, as the newspapers did yesterday, 45-year-old hiker Dave Scott "Some walkers are grateful for the sit-down, but then you end up reading the brass plaque on the bench and it's all a bit depressing."

Bloody stroll-on, is both my reaction and my advice. Oh, look, here comes rambling Dave Scott, striding cheerily westward in his big stout boots and his big nubbly socks on this fine pre-vernal morning, his heart is light, his smile is broad, for he has heard a lark on the wing, he has spotted a snail on the thorn, and it is borne in upon him that since God is patently in His heaven and all's right with the World, this would be the ideal moment for a bit of a sit-down and a squint at the sun-dappled bay of St Bride's while he nibbles a chunk of the Kendal Mint Cake he always keeps tucked into the clever little pocket he has had specially sewn into his bobbled hat. But, hang about, what is this? As Dave gratefully lowers his corduroy rump on to the friendly plank, that keen snail-spotting eye of his clocks a plaque informing him that the bench is dedicated to the memory of Trevor Foskett, beloved dad, grandpa, friend, and award-winning postman, who, having passed this lovely spot so many times, has now passed on to an even lovelier.

Immediately, for sensitive Mr Scott, the lark trills a bum note, the snail sucks in its head, and the sun clouds over into glum Celtic twilight. God may still be in His heaven, but now that Dave has discovered He has got Trevor

Foskett up there with Him, all's wrong with the world.

Do you know, I had really believed that ramblers were whittled from stouter timber? I speak as one who has watched them go quite literally from strength to strength over recent years as, newly empowered with the right to roam and ranks and funding exponentially swelling, they moved inexorably forward behind the fearsome Boadicea Street-Porter into any broad sunlit uplands that happened to take their fancy, prepared to knock seven bells out of anyone who stood in the way of their life, liberty, and the pursuit of grid references. More yet, I had always assumed that a proximity to Mother Nature far closer than the national norm would have accustomed all these battle-hardened ramblers to her funny little ways – not only is the countryside full of death, it couldn't continue to be the countryside without it: something has to kick up the daisies. So I cannot for the life of me see why intimations of mortality should have Dave Scott uncontrollably burying his sodden face in the red-spotted hankie I would have expected to remain on the end of his stick until it was time to unwrap his pork pie.

Especially when a nice brass plaque is itself something of a hedge against that mortality: is it not cheering, Mr Scott, to think that there is some corner of a Pembroke field that is forever Foskett? Is it not statistically possible that since more than a million people visit the Pembrokeshire Coast National Park every year, at least some of them at some time will have said to one another "Tell you what, just for a change, you ramble that way, I'll ramble this, and – synchronise watches, tighten Thermoses – we'll meet up at Foskett's Bench at two pip emma for a mug of Bovril"?

Indeed, still but a callow 45-year-old, you may not yet

appreciate that the day might well come, a few rambling decades hence, when you yourself – having had a bit more time to observe that full many a flower is born to blush unseen and waste its sweetness on the Pembroke air – will hanker after something rustproof bolted solidly on to a coastal wastebin in imperishable testimony that "Dave Scott once chucked a rucksackful of used Kleenex into this fine receptacle, but, rest assured, fellow rambler he is a lot happier now."

All A Bit Hairy

YOU who have loyally been dropping marmalade on me down the long arches of the years and therefore know me to be a political commentator with his finger on the pulse and his ear to the ground – picture a Sioux cardiologist and you will not be far out – may have sometimes found yourself puzzling over the fact that I have never written about Gerhard Schröder.

There is a very good reason for this. It concerns the umlaut: you cannot type an umlaut on a computer keyboard without summoning up something from what I believe is called a menu, using that titchy arrow which scuttles about on the electronic end of your mouse. When you have summoned it up, you hunt the umlaut, and when you have found it you do the mouse-arrow thing again and the umlaut miraculously migrates, so that when you get your text back on-screen, there it is, hovering over the letter that was crying out for it. I was shown how to do all this when the man came with my computer, but after the man went away again I forgot what he said, because there was a ton of stuff more important to remember than how to find the thing that did umlauts. Then, after a month or so, I was banging out a travel piece about Venezuela and found myself in sudden need of one of those squiggles Hispanophones jot over letters to enable them to enunciate *mañana* – there it is now – so I rang up the man and he talked me through it again (much in the manner of a control tower when a pilot has passed out at the joystick and the luckless Learjet has to be landed by Michael Winner), and *mañana* came out bang on, ie, with the squiggle bang on it. So I thought I had the hang of it, now; until the next time, when it was an umlaut I needed and after about half an hour's oathful struggle, I finally got back my text to discover that the targeted u did not have an umlaut on top of it, it had a circumflex. Which was when I concluded that life was too short for this kind of thing, a deadline is a deadline and a consummate professional like me is not going to miss *Countdown* just to get some foreign bloody word diacritically spot-on; especially when there were so many different spots to get on, or, indeed, under, and, in a number of Scandinavian cases, through.

Thus it was that whenever Chancellor Schröder did anything, I let someone else tell you about it, happy to leave it to some dab hand at computers who knew exactly where to dab his hand to get the umlauts in by tea-time. It didn't bother me much, as it turned out, because Gerhard didn't do much to bother me: certainly, his has been a Kanzleramt unremarkable for anything worth the risk of missing Carol Vorderman slapping a vowel up. Until, that is, and as you will by now have gathered, today: today (I shall now stop typing his surname, or, never mind *Countdown*, I shall miss *Newsnight*), Gerhard did something to make thy knotted and combined locks to part, and each particular hair to stand on end, like quills upon the fretful porpentine, a quotation selected with more than customary heavyhandedness: for what Gerhard did was, and I quote "fly into a rage and threaten to sue anyone who accused him of dyeing his hair", an accusation which, it seems, has been made in a number of newspapers over the past few days.

Unsettling, eh? Has your own hair come down yet, or is it still struggling to cope with the shattering news that a hitherto calm, rational, controlled – or whatever other handle you care to choose for dull – German leader, can fly off that handle at the merest suggestion that his barnet may perhaps have had the decorators in? If that is your risen hair's concern, I sympathise – hair may not know much, but it knows about hair, and it therefore knows that, before Gerhard, there were just three other German leaders who were tonsorially manic: there was Otto von Bismarck, whose egregious muttonchops were not only given a going-over three times each day by a barber kept constantly within earshot but also put to bed in individual pomaded muslin bags; there was Kaiser Wilhelm II, whose black moustaches were waxed at right angles and of such a height as to form a shimmering trident with the polished spike of his Pickelhaube; and there was the one with the forelock-and-toothbrush set designed to last for a thousand years, even when wet, but which tragically fell somewhat short, leaving the restorative market open for a grateful Graham Gooch.

Not, perhaps, the three German leaders with whom you and I would choose to sit down for a hand of bridge; but does that mean we should worry about the one who, in this hairy respect, makes up a fourth? No: you and I have enough to worry about with Lord Bragg. Thank God he hasn't got an umlaut.

Near Myth

BRITISH *package-tourists, complains the Greek Ministry of Tourism, have no interest in the country's culture. Easily remedied, I'd have thought: why not just update a few pithy myths? Like, say, the Twelve Labours of Hercules...*

Prolegomenon: Hercules (né Heracles) was the greatest of the Greek heroes. He was often worshipped as a god, but his name shows that he was a man, since it means "glorious gift of Hera" and no divine name in Greek is thus compounded of another deity's name. Also, he had a car.

He was born to Alcmena and her husband Amphitryon, although there is strong evidence that he was fathered by Zeus while Amphitryon was away, trying to make a go of a kebab house in Chalk Farm. He was, however, raised by

Amphitryon upon the latter's return to Thebes, and grew to be very strong, thereby attracting the attention of Eurystheus of Mycenae, the legendary travel agent and topless bouzouki bar mogul. It was for him that Hercules performed the 12 great tasks forever associated with his name. Here are five. Those wishing to read all 12 will have to book full-board.

Hercules and the Bore of Erymanthus: It happened that Eurystheus, ever mindful to expand, built at Erymanthus in the Peloponnesus a great complex, fashioned in sturdy breeze-block and finished in sensible vomit-hued emulsion with unbreakable furniture, capable of housing 1,200 Britons per week, well away from civilised people.

At first, it was packed; then people began to cancel in droves, none knew why. At last, word reached Eurystheus concerning a horrendous beast who was waylaying visitors to the MacOedipus Eaterie and driving them crazy with anecdotes about his room extension in Walsall. Hercules was alerted, and appeared to the man in the guise of a Jehovah's Double-Glazier whose friends had told him he was funnier than Bernard Manning. After 19 hours of continuous hectoring, the Bore of Erymanthus jumped out of the window onto the rocks beneath, where the gods turned him into a big red stain.

Hercules triumphs over Cerberus: Once, at the Oresteian Gift Boutique in Skios, a Barnet man bought a model of Cerberus the many-headed dog for the rear shelf of his Mondeo, but quickly took it back. "Oy, you filthy dago toerag," he explained to the proprietor, "only five of its little heads nod!" At this, Hercules – who had been delivering a crate of Clytemnestra whistling diaphragms – reached out with the grace of a god and smacked the dog on the rump. Immediately, not only did all nine heads begin nodding, but also, by some miracle, its 18 eyes lit up.

Hercules overcomes the giant Essexwoman: Legend has it that one morning near Delphi, at The Oracle In A Basket, a big woman from Chigwell complained of garlic on her chips. In the ensuing fracas, she felled three waiters, a Minotours guide, and an elderly Runcorn couple queuing for a ticket to Anne Homer's Cottage. Desperate, the restaurateur summoned Hercules who, not wishing to wreak further damage, instead removed his wig, gave her a lollipop, and murmured: "Who loves ya, baby?" The big woman from Chigwell swooned, and could be strapped to the roof of the charabanc with no bother at all.

Hercules and the Augean stables: It came upon the nonce that a group of young heroes, deeply disturbed by the failure of Chelsea to win the away leg against Kindergarten Dortmund, spent the next few months wandering around Europe, raping and pillaging.

At last, having been cast adrift by Venetian police in an open gondola, they washed up on the shores of Stassounopoulos, where Eurystheus had recently built a chipboard paradise called the Augean Leisure Complex'n'Legoverama. Advancing up the beach, shrieking and whipping open their raincoats as they ran, the heroes presented something of a problem for Hercules, there by chance to help Russell Crowe and Lee Bowyer judge that week's Geri Halliwell Singalike Dog Contest, since the hotel was fully booked.

He found himself with no other course but to lodge them in the Augean stables. It proved to be one of his rare failures: true, the Chelsea supporters were happy enough, but when they moved on after a week, the horses refused to go back inside for six months.

The Causeway of Hercules: Just off the island of Lemnos, there is a strange outcrop of small brown hummocks that seem to have been flung out into the sea by some mighty hand. Legend has it that they once belonged to a party of lousy tippers from Birkenhead who asked Hercules to carry their luggage.

Enough to Drive You Mad

I HAD a little window on Monday morning, when, for a few fleet seconds, there was nothing to worry about. That is the trouble with seconds; they fleet. The little window was both real and metaphorical: it is the topmost window of my tall thin house, and it looks down from my attic sweatshop into my garden, which is so far below that you need binoculars to see whether frost has got the geraniums. The thing is, it dropped below zero on Sunday night, but I didn't know this until I had climbed upstairs to type and spotted rime on the cars outside; so I took my binoculars off the binocular-shelf and focused them on my distant tubs but the geraniums had not gone black beneath the polythene cauls designed to keep them snug, and I did not have to worry about them any more. So I shut the real window, and picked up *The Times*, and immediately the metaphorical window shut, too: I started worrying about lying half-naked, at the age of 73, under a hedge near Hampton Lucy.

Hampton Lucy is not a woman. I agree that the sentence would be far more intriguing if it were, but there is nothing I can do about that. Hampton Lucy is a village. I started worrying because *The Times* reported that the Commission for Integrated Transport had delivered a recommendation that, in order simultaneously to penalise and ease congestion, black boxes containing smart payment-cards be fitted to every car in Britain by 2012, linked to Global Positioning System satellites, so that motorists could be charged for every mile they drove on major roads at peak times. This sentence, everyone will immediately spot, contains nine different things to worry about, but everyone will not have spotted the thing about Hampton Lucy's hedge. It is just me who spotted that.

Or, rather, spotted that a typical impost – driving from London to Rugby on the M1 – would be £3.40, whereas doing the trip on minor roads, at off-peak times, would be free. Now, I don't know how much money I shall have by 2012, but as I shall be relying on pensions from companies that will on present actuarial reckoning almost certainly have gone bust (including HM Government), I know that I shall not have £3.40 to chuck away on a luxury rush-hour trip up the Ml, especially as the £3.40 will probably be 600 euros by then. If I want to go to Rugby (I have not yet visited it, and old men need hobbies) I shall, at 73, have to crawl into my clapped-out banger, and, with Mrs Coren holding the map, set out on minor roads. At an off-peak time. Leaving, that is to say, our council lean-to (the tall thin house having been repossessed, see income statement above) after nightfall – if, of course, we have managed to hobble to the car and unlocked the door with our arthritic mittened fingers without being pounced on by muggers, smackheads, bangerjackers and whoever else has come along by then to plague the lives of the last three coppers in London – and set off on what I see from the atlas beside me is the A4146 to Leighton Buzzard. Whether Mrs Coren will be able to see that in 2012, in a pitch-dark car is, however, another matter: though far younger than I, she might easily need specs by then, which – following the NHS privatisation that sets their cost at 600 euros a pair, could well have been borrowed from a friend with somewhat different refraction – may not enable her even to find the right page on the map, let alone identify the titchy numerals. We could end up, two days later, staring out over Land's End.

But even if she manages it, those two days might still not take us much nearer Rugby than, say, Yardley Gobion. Why on earth would it take you two days to reach Yardley Gobion, you may wonder, when it is surely only a mile or two from Grafton Regis? I think you have forgotten that the Commission for Integrated Transport is bent on ensuring that all but the rich keep to the minor roads: while the motorways will be carrying only a handful of Rollers and Aston-Martins hither and yon, the spindly little byways all over the atlas beside me will be clogged nose-to-tail, all night, with the country's hapless impoverished, struggling to get to Rugby or wherever. And, what is worse, having to push their cars off the road as dawn comes up, for fear of the Global Positioning System satellite clocking them driving during peak-time.

You can see how it might take a week to get to Hampton Lucy. And how I could end up half-naked, lying under a hedge. I couldn't sleep six nights in a car-seat with the way my back will be by 2012, and I'm not going to kip under a hedge in my clothes, am l? Not if I want to arrive in Rugby looking smart. I just hope it isn't as bloody freezing as it was on Sunday night.

Chinese Whispers

TODAY, as you will be all too aware, is the 75th anniversary of the founding of the English Table Tennis Association. Not only will this milestone event be celebrated throughout the queendom in the time-honoured tradition, with high teas served at wonky trestle tables under which the hard-boiled eggs will be rolled so that celebrants on all fours will be encouraged to bang their heads, and cry "Ow!" as their forbears have been doing since that first fateful day in 1927, but it will also be written about by me. I shall not be writing about all of it, however, since the history of table tennis is so bizarrely rich and richly bizarre in incident and anecdote that any attempt to grasp its myriad oddities can only result, as we shall imminently see, in the topic suddenly bouncing off unpredictably in all directions and either ending up anywhere or disappearing completely, most frequently both.

To begin with, table tennis is responsible for not only the most glaring but also the most mystifying error in the *Oxford English Dictionary*. Look up the word ping-pong and you will read that the word is "imitative of the sound of a bat striking a ball". No it isn't. You and I have played many games of table tennis (though not, sadly, together), and neither of us has ever heard anything go either ping or pong. What the anything goes is either tick or tock, depending on the force deployed. Now, it's no good the *Oxford English Dictionary* arguing "yes, we know that, we are not fools up here in Great Clarendon Street, we have been in this business a long time, but the fact of the matter is that tick-tock was already spoken for", because it is their job to explain why ping-pong was coined, since it couldn't be onomatopoeic unless the game was originally played on a tin table with brass bats and a little spherical gong, which it patently wasn't. Not of course that I've tried this, I wouldn't know where to begin, but there are times when common sense should be fallen back on, as the *OED* would do well to recognise.

My personal etymological take is that since table tennis is China's most popular game – cribbage coming a poor second – ping and pong almost certainly derive from ying and yang, the passive female and active male principles of the universe, which, conjoined, form a ball. That they are also the words for female and male genitalia need not detain us here, unless we happen to know the noise they make; but since I don't, and common sense is for once no help, let me instead endorse this reading both by pointing out that table tennis is a game combining defence (passive) with offence (active) and by reminding you that Rupert Bear's dog was a Pekinese called Ping-Pong. Am I alone in being astonished that the *OED*, upon which several thousand researchers have worked for more than a century, have failed to clock any of this? Especially when there is also, I have heard, an unpublished *Just-So* story entitled "How The Pekinese Got A Flat Face", which describes how one palace pet ran off with the ball in the middle of a crucial match between the Emperor Chung-Su and Concubine 197, and got reprimanded with a furious imperial forehand smash.

Which, I think, brings me to the point where I should stop hundreds of you from writing in to inquire whether King Kong is (a) onomatopoeic, and/or (b) anything to do with table tennis. The answers are (a) how the hell should I know, why not go out and listen to a gorilla? and (b) only obliquely, given that the Danish for King Kong is, remarkably, Kong King. Where the obliqueness comes in is that it was at the Battle of Copenhagen, in 1801, that Horatio Nelson famously put his telescope to his blind eye and announced: "I see no ships". You, of course, already know this, but what you may not know is that, after the battle was over, with the Danish fleet sunk, Nelson's grog-sodden crew were somewhat erratically dancing a celebratory hornpipe when the little admiral suddenly appeared among them in a forgivably jocular mood and removed his eye-patch, revealing not an empty socket but a ping-pong ball on which the ship's scrivener had quilled the word "Gotcha!"

What is not quite so certain is whether the sharp divide between players who use the shake-hand grip and those who use the penholder has anything to do with class: it has when it comes to knives and forks, but bats are a puzzle, especially given that it is the Chinese who favour the penholder, even though cutlery is a closed book to them.

NB: One of Dame Barbara Cartland's many Pekinese was called Mister Wu, but since she almost certainly named him in honour of George Formby's laundry man, I am inclined to doubt that this has much to do with table tennis. Although one can never be sure; it's a funny old game.

All In the Mind

YES, of course, why not, wasn't it inevitable that television would eventually get round to dumbing down intelligence itself? And don't we all know where, in our wonderful enterprise culture, things go from here?

Look at this. It hit my mat this very morning. It is Desmond Guccione's brand new magazine, *Mensa Only*, and it has fallen open at the shimmering gatefold showing the gorgeous left cerebral hemisphere of the ex-Roedean stunner with the voluptuous 166 IQ, Brainmate of the Month Melinda van Jordan. "Even at 14, I was amazingly developed for my age," she says, "and it was only a matter of time before I caught the eye of our fabulous young science master. He was an absolute dish, with this enormous domed head, probably a seven-and-seven-eighths, and in fact my first thought was, gosh, am I biting off more than I can chew here, I've only messed around with kids before? But he was very gentle, very understanding, and pretty soon I was sneaking out of my dorm in the small hours, and we'd make intense, passionate conversation for hours on end across his desk. It was terrific! He gave me everything I'd ever expected from thinking, it was all I'd hoped for and more. He wanted me to run away with him and do unified theory in Tahiti, and I almost went. But suddenly I realised I was only just beginning to live: once I'd discovered thinking was so – ooh, you know! – I wanted to try it with lots of other men. And after we parted, I did. I don't regret it for a moment; it's only small-minded people who disapprove of a girl who thinks around. My fave turn-ons? I love solid state physics, of course, and Aramaic textual cruces, and Beethoven's *Diabelli Variations*, but best of all is – wow! – medieval Balkan diplomacy."

But *Mensa Only* is not targeted just at male geniuses. Flipping the page, I find a tastefully embossed banner headline offering any woman taking out an annual subscription a Giant Inflatable Bertrand Russell Doll. Beneath, runs this irresistible text: "Yes, it's true! At last, an end to those long lonely nights with nobody to bounce your ideas off! At last, an intellectual equal who won't be forever chipping in with his own revolutionary philosophical concepts! At last, a stunning companion you can take along to the most genius-packed party without worrying that some hot-shot PhD motormouth will steal him away to the car park to discuss Hegelian loopholes!

"Bertrand Russell comes in a flat pack no bigger than a

cigar-box and may be slipped unobtrusively into your handbag for that sneaky weekend in Heidelberg, or even a quickie overnight seminar in Balliol. No hotel manager is going to raise an eyebrow when you take Bertrand Russell upstairs, where, in the snug privacy of your room, you just blow him up to the size required and start talking! He's made out of durable, washable, non-iron heavy-duty poly-thene with a choice of hats, and he's yours at the unbeatable price of £9.95 (inc VAT) when you take out a subscription. Also available: Wittgenstein, Kierkegaard, Alfred North Whitehead, and, for beginners, Michael Parkinson."

Turn the page yet again, and there is a complete short story entitled *Hot for Hermeneutics*, in which four Somerville undergraduates and one fantastically endowed All Souls don (he has a Regius Professorship, an Ecclestone Fellowship, two Hinduja bursaries, and a Cary grant) put it all together over a long weekend locked in the Bodleian, during which the girls begin by trying to persuade him that Shakespeare was Thomas Kyd and end up continued on page 192, which I have not yet done on account of I had to go and lie down with a wet flannel on my head.

Nor, lest the public be misled into assuming that all this unfettered cerebration is aimed at single thinkers only, are married couples forgotten. Apart from the hundreds of tasteful fuzzy Polaroids, mindbending thumbnail vignettes, and invaluable box numbers of Thinkers' Wives, Meta-physicians' Husbands, and Swinging Rationalist Couples, the magazine has a full page of informed and sympathetic advice to those out of whose dialectic the magic has somehow gone. Typically, this appears alongside an advertisement from Dolores Glamour Thinking Ltd for what is described as a French Existentialist Set, comprising a three-piece charcoal grey pinstripe suit (state male/female/both, when ordering) covered in simulated Gauloise ash and absinthe stains, a pair of naughty pince-nez,three of Jean-Paul Sartre's see-through propositions and a revealing split syllogism which is yours to examine for seven days, whether or not you decide to keep the entire outfit.

Forgive me, readers, but I must break off now. The wet flannel being all steamed out, I am ready to turn to page 192. And after that, perhaps, the very short interview with John Prescott.

The Invisible Man

THEY are all gone into the world of light, and I alone sit lingering here – a hell of a lot more irritably, I don't mind saying, than Henry Vaughan, thanks to the fact that while Henry, three centuries back, had no option but to come to terms with being left lingering, I had been led to believe that I possessed the wondrous wherewithal to whiz off into the world of light, track down my dear departed, and sit lingering here, possibly for hours, growing less alone with every passing minute as ancestor after ancestor swam into my ken. I had a computer. More yet, I had the address of a website, set up for me and millions of like-minded bereaved by a company called

Qinetiq, which, working in collaboration with BT and twigging that the world of light was but another name for cyberspace, had put the 1901 census within reach of everyone with a laptop.

Until everyone discovered that the grasp exceeded the reach. More fool everyone: we should have known what to expect when a company not only chooses to christen itself Qinetiq because it looks much sassier than Kinetic, but also clasps to its bosom a technological sidekick which has trouble connecting you with 999, never mind 1901; and it should thus have come as no surprise that BT was unable to cope with the demand on its new service. Last Friday, I rushed upstairs, logged on, went off with a pitterpatting heart to find grandpa, got to within a Sistine fingertip, and then the world of light crashed. Too many, it seemed, had wanted to find their own grandpas.

Four days on, I still sit lingering here alone, like a sap at a seance: my grandpa is out there, somewhere, I am desperate to make contact, but my medium cannot crack it. Madame Apple is unable to get in touch with the other side. Now, you will say: ease up, be cool, why are you so desperate to scroll up grandpa's records, you will find nothing you do not know, the census will tell you merely that in 1901 Harry Coren was 15 years old, lived in Hoxton, and worked as a Billingsgate fish-porter. Ah, yes, I reply, but what of his brother? What brother, you say? The brother nobody talks about, of course.

Let us roll forward from January 1901 to January 1978, which we can also roll back to without need of Qinetiq, because I was there, then, at grandpa's funeral, where my large family was standing around, suitably sad, but also saying "93, a good innings" to all and sundry. Well, not quite to all and sundry; for there, at the graveside, beside grandpa's seven daughters and sons, stood a very old man, to whom nobody was saying anything at all. I had never seen him before, although when I saw him now, I might have been forgiven for thinking I had; indeed, I might have been forgiven for fainting away at that thought, because he was a dead ringer for my grandfather. Or, rather, a live ringer. Who was he? Where had he come from? Who could say, because nobody would. I nudged my father, who shook his head. I nudged my mother, who put a finger to her lips, and an uncle, who frowned, and an aunt, who looked at her gloves.

Well, we lowered grandpa away, and did the thing with the handful of dust, and we convoyed back to grandpa's house, and everyone drank, and everyone snacked, and everyone talked. Except the man who wasn't there. I tried to ask about the man who wasn't there, and everyone said what man, did you see a man, I didn't see a man, nor did I; so I stood around, 40 years old, practically grown up, the eldest grandchild what's more, but nobody would tell me anything about the man who wasn't there.

He is there now, though. In the world of light I cannot get to. I know that, because, when I pressed the point driving home from the cemetery, my father finally sighed and said the man was your grandfather's brother, but nobody talks about him, we turn left here, mind that van. And that was all there ever was, which is why I ache to log on. For there was another Coren in Harry's Hoxton house (an aitchless address in 1901, but – yes, I went there for clues – a poncy installation gallery now), and I need that Coren's name. If I find his name, I may be able to find more, especially the more that made him the man of whom nobody spoke – will that name perhaps be trackable to some yellowed Met file of whoremongers, arsonists, Wipers deserters? Was he an oppo of Doctor Crippen, or Gavrilo Prinzip, or Horatio Bottomley? Or was he merely – for it has just occurred to me that my family was straiter-laced, back then – one of Oscar's bits of East End rough?

I hear what you say: let sleeping websites lie. I'll take that chance: a little learning may be a dangerous thing, but lingering alone can drive you nuts.

Going to the Dogs

WHO was the most decorated German of the First World War? Rin Tin Tin. This will come as no surprise, of course, to those of you who knew it, but if you knew only that Rin Tin Tin was a dog, I trust your gob is suitably smacked. His name was not Rin Tin Tin at the time, mind, he changed it when he went to Hollywood, much like Kirk Douglas (one fake name self-plucked from umpteen – popping into the head, I suspect, only because Kirk and Rin are almost indistinguishably vulpine) but when he fought on the Western Front, he was not only as German a shepherd as you could shake a stick at, he stood up to so much more than shaken sticks that by the time Siegfried Sassoon suddenly burst out singing, the alsatian on the other side of no man's land had totted up 17 medals for gallantry. He did not wear them, of course, because, faced with a dog that tough, the Kaiser would forgivably have shrunk from pinning anything on him, let alone kissing him on both cheeks, but Germany's greatest hero was what he was. He then went off to be a movie star, leaving a nation so bereft that Corporal Hitler immediately clocked how this bitter blow might someday be turned to his advantage.

Which brings me, as you may have guessed, to the even more dispiriting news that the British Army is finding it extremely difficult to recruit dogs. Dogs have ever been integral to the very warp and, er, woof of our military might: to quote the senior officer who has just gone public on this grave national emergency, "Dogs have by tradition kept coming from the same places, rather like service families, with sons following fathers into the forces," but they are not now coming as they used to. The type of British dog who counted service and loyalty to Queen and country above all else is not signing up as heretofore, and the news has laid me low.

You who have no shrapnel collection with which to fascinate your friends and illuminate your thrilling tales of Anderson shelter and Mickey Mouse gasmask, who did not stand on Euston Station with a label pinned to your balaclava directing you to Blackpool's remote sanctuary, will not recall the island race of plucky dogs who, when Neville Chamberlain quavered his drear message on the September wirelesses, dropped their bones, unplugged their conks from one another's tails, and rallied, as one dog, to the flag of this beleaguered country. By the end of 1939 there were 20,000 serving dogs prepared not to reason why. But now? Apparently, the alsatian – on which the services have always most relied – is not the dog it was: it has become less amenable to discipline, less unquestioningly loyal; order it to charge into the Valley of Death, and it might very well bark a canine expletive and take a chunk out of you.

What has brought this on? Take your pick: collapse of authority in the home, caring lefty trainers pledged to encourage self-expression in dog-school and sparing the rod for fear of winding up before the Strasbourg beaks, working mums employing amateur dogminders who leave their charges lying beside hot radiators all day watching Rolf Harris instead of taking them out for long brisk walks, gourmet food enriched with this and that replacing the healthy chase of an agile rat, fat-dog salaries for cushy jobs in security and modelling and tellysoaps and bog-roll promotion, canine coiffeurs and poop-scoops and Good Boy chocs and psychotherapists and masseurs and Burberry weskits and all the other kitschy paraphernalia of spoiled softydom – should we be surprised that a generation of dogs has grown up for whom yomping through enemy lines on a diet of leftover bully, stormed at with shot and shell for no more tangible reward than some corner of a foreign field and a valedictory bugle, is some-thing less than the career of choice?

To whom, then, should we turn in our hour of doggy need? Where else but to him who has taught us that there is nowhere else to turn? A national hero committed to internationalising that heroism for the selfless sake of Queen and country, whose dog would be looked up to by every other British dog, if only he had one. Indeed, I am astonished that he still hasn't, given that the man he admires on this side idolatry, and possibly that side, too,

118

owned nationally dutiful dogs who, after he was all but terminally pretzelled, not only helped to save his life but virtually guaranteed his second term. If Mr Blair took a leaf out of George W's book, and got himself a brave and obedient pooch who would trot devotedly at his heel wherever that heel took its endless peregrinations, who could not believe that this would bring all other British dogs to their patriotic senses?

Either that or step aside for Blunkett.

Stocking Up

DEAR Santa: I realise that this is an unorthodox means of contacting you. I accept that the sensible procedure would be to put this letter in an envelope and post it to Lapland, I think it is, could be Greenland, addressed to Santa Santasson, the name I assume you go by up there – God knows how Scandinavians ever get any letters at all when they all have the same name, it must be because they are delivered by elves, not only famously helpful but also with useful recourse to magic if there is, say, a go-slow up the sorting office. But it is very different down here in Consignia, where I am now forced to live my postal life, because the Consignians are bloody diabolical when it comes to delivering letters, Santa. You stick something in one of their pillarboxes and chances are nobody ever sees it again, let alone in time for Christmas.

It is not, however, postal unreliability alone that has persuaded me to this open public letter, it is also the fact that you do not exist – no offence meant, but it has long been my view that anyone who puts a mince pie and a glass of Tio Pepe on his mantelpiece in gratitude for the nice new top-of-the-range chainsaw he expects to come down his chimney is likely to be eating his next Christmas lunch in Broadmoor. So this letter is nothing but a ruse: it is the means whereby friends and relatives, currently racking their brains over what to buy me, may see my wish-list. So then...

I should like one of those things you can buy which shows you where the easy-pull strip is on Cellophane wrapping, so that you don't end up – having sheared a couple of fingernails – chewing it off your new CD/tissue-pack/gas-station sandwich, etc. If you can afford it, I'd most like the one that has a little attachment showing you where the pre-weakened notch is on packets so that you don't have to apologise for popcorn or crisps all over people. I should, it goes without saying, like the model that also has a tiny little thing on it that not only seeks out the end of a half-used Sellotape roll but also enables you, once it has shown you where it is, to avoid pulling the tape off in little thin strips, but I don't think this model is available in Europe, yet.

I should like one of those things you can buy which rings a bell to warn you that you have shut your coat in the car door and a bit of it is hanging out. This is not to be confused with the one you can buy which rings a bell when you have shut your seatbelt in the car door and think you are being strangled by someone who has got into the back seat. I don't want one of those, for personal reasons.

What I do want, though, is one of those things you can buy that collects up all the fragments of toenail that whiz all over the room during cutting. I should prefer the clockwork one to the electric model, if that's all right, because I should not want to find that the battery had suddenly run out when people were coming for dinner.

I should also like one of those things you can buy which has a little red light on a combined hook and rubber band-type of arrangement which may be attached to anything such as a wine glass or a TV remote control or a watch or a Mars bar or anything else you put on the carpet when lying there reading and then leave when you have to go out of the room and then tread on when you come back in. The little red light flashes on and off to warn you. I do not want the top-of-the-range version you can buy which can also be attached to a gerbil or iguana, because I don't have anything of that nature, and it would just be chucking good money away.

If, however, you are one of my friends or relatives who does not mind splashing out a bit, it is after all only once a year, I should really like one of those things you can buy which is probably best described as a plastic half-eaten breadstick containing an ultrasonic whistle, tuned to a pitch that can be picked up only by the ears of waiters: should you wish to attract a waiter's attention, simply remove what looks like a half-eaten breadstick from its handy carrying-case, put it to your lips as if biting it, but blow instead. I am told that the audio-gearing is so precise that it has never been known to bring either dogs or whales into a restaurant, but, should this happen, there is a full money-back warranty.

Now the tricky bit: if, Santa, you do exist, then obviously I'd hate to offend you. Therefore, were you of a mind to chip in with a token stocking-filler, I should like one of those things you can buy that, when you are pushing an aspirin, beta-blocker, vitamin, or other fine pill from its snug little home in a blister-pack, catches it before it flies out and rolls under the sideboard. There'll be plenty of stockists in Lapland, I'm sure. Or Greenland.

Rudolf the Nose-Job Reindeer

L AST time, I tried your patience by selfishly deploying my keyboard to tell my loved ones what I wanted for Christmas. This time, I must run the risk of trying it yet further by telling them – because this has suddenly become even more important – what I don't want.

I don't want any lip. Much less do I want any nose. And don't let the ambiguous vagaries of our language mislead you: when I say that I don't want any nose, I don't mean that I don't want just any old nose, I don't mean that running down on Christmas morning and finding a really terrific nose under the tree would thrill and delight me, I really do mean that I don't want any nose at all. Although a glance at the snapshot on the dust jacket might question my taste, I am happy with the nose I've got. Also, both ears, though you can see only one; the other one is, if you can imagine it, a sort of mirror image, and I am very happy with the matched pair of them, and how far out they currently stick. I am not, mind, quite as happy with the chins you will find at the bottom of the picture, especially when I recall the days when there was only one and it was nowhere near the bottom, but there again, I am content enough with the current crop not to want them chopped off and chopped in for a new lantern-jawed model, possibly from their ever-popular Kirk Douglas range, by the Harley Medical Group.

You see? All you had to do was wait, that is what trying patience is all about, and now you know that my topic today is drawn from the recent report that the HMG has launched a range of gift vouchers for plastic surgery, so that loved ones may give one another everything from cheap and cheerful collagen lip implants right up to the full and highly expensive Monty. "Whether it be a group of friends clubbing together for a pal's first Botox injections, or a breast reduction for your mother," declared Diana Hansen, described as a Harley Medical Group spokesman, "the motives for giving the vouchers are endless."

You bet they are, Diana. Even as I speculate as to why you are described as a spokesman, I accept that the motives for wanting surgical interference with one's nearest and dearest are literally endless, now we have entered an era when the end of anything can be lessened, or indeed augmented, at will. All that bothers me is the will itself: for while it is one thing for me to make my own decision to brave the combing challenge of having my pubic hair transplanted into the dome you can also see in the snapshot, it is quite another for a group of friends to club together to ensure they are no longer seen in embarrassingly slap-head company. As to the trickiness of composing a message to go with Ms Hansen's charming latter suggestion – "Merry Christmas, Mum, and Happy New Tits!" perhaps – it is nothing compared to what a man would have to come up with when buying a set for his significant other, especially if she is spectacularly significant and has, moreover, always been happy that way. If, of course, she is spectacularly insignificant, but had always believed her partner loved her that way, then a Yuletide voucher for a set of 38 Double-Ds might go down very badly; the more so if, a few short months later, they themselves go down very badly.

We must also address, Diana, the problem of the general public's medical naivety: there are people who, unable to afford a voucher for the lifting of two buttocks, will buy a voucher for just the one, promising a second next Christmas. The luckless recipient, not wanting to hurt the giver's feelings, will then be doomed to an uncomfortable and unsightly asymmetric year; unless, of course, the clinic is willing to exchange the buttock voucher for half a dozen crow's feet and a couple of dimples. I am also concerned at the stir your promotion might have created among the nation's millions of dimwit DIY enthusiasts, who – unable to afford a professional job but unwilling to see loved ones go without – may resort to their Black & Deckers in a caring bid to give their kids a nose they'd be proud to blow. Furthermore, it would be irresponsible for a major social commentator to minimise the risks attendant upon amateur liposuction: I have seen the current TV ads for the powerful new Dyson, and am now stuck with the image of a devoted infant coming upon its dozing grannie and, wishing to give her a really special present, emptying her entire contents with a single suck.

Still, 'tis the season to be charitable, so when I wish you all a very merry Christmas, that includes the Harley Medical Group. When it comes to a prosperous new year, however, that's just you.

Bored Games

BACKGAMMON is played with a big black leather carrying-case garnished with sterling silver hinges and containing 30 genuine bone men, two ivory dice, and an ormolu-mounted rosewood beaker to shake them in. The first player suggests that someone might like a game, and goes out to his car to collect the case. While he is out, the second player runs and gets his monogrammed Gucci set from the host's coat-cupboard and has it open by the time the first player returns, revealing it to contain 30 antique ivory pieces, two solid gold dice (to match the case's hinges), and a George III cow-creamer to shake them in. The first player then stares at it and falls silent, leaving the challenge to be taken up by a third player who smilingly removes from his breast-pocket a solid gold Asprey & Garrard carrying-case containing a travelling backgammon board, 30 platinum counters and a miniature computer fed with a random program in lieu of dice.

This game continues until it is won by a man who produces an old boxwood backgammon set stuck together with Elastoplast and given to him by his nanny in 1959, ie, some 40-odd years before the present craze started.

MONOPOLY is a game for any number of players. Its rules are very simple: the Monopoly board is opened, and the first player cries: "My God, will you look at that, things have changed a bit since the days when you could buy a house on Park Lane for two hundred quid, haw, haw, haw, has that ever occurred to anyone else here?" The player on his left then shrieks: "Never mind that, what about the whole of Regent Street for three hundred? It's just cost me that to have my bloody car clamped outside Liberty's!" To this, the next player shouts: "Tell you one thing, though, tell you one thing, would you pay two hundred for a privatised bloody wossname, station, am I right or am I wrong, tuppence more like, I say tuppence more like!" The turn having come round to the first player again, he picks up a Community Chest card and screams: "No, wait, listen to this, *listen to this*, pay school fees of one hundred and fifty pounds, ho, ho, I wish, stone me, when I think what I have to fork out every term for..."

The game goes on until the last player has bored himself to death.

SCRABBLE is a vicious game of bluff and psychology played with a board and letters on premises where there is no access to a dictionary. The object is to embarrass one's opponents into accepting more and more unlikely words until your score is beyond reach. If, for example, you receive letters YLUGXOQ, you must very quickly, and with a triumphant cry – lay down the word GLOXQUY, claiming a face value of 27 points (doubled or trebled whenever possible), plus 50-point bonus for getting rid of all your seven letters. Challenged, you reply that a gloxquy was a small feathered instrument for wiping the reed of a shawm. This process is repeated until all letters, and indeed all players, are exhausted.

NB: Should anyone try this on you, on no account lose your temper. The correct objection when faced with an opponent's GLOXQUY is a light chuckle, a despairing shake of the head, and a gentle remonstration to the effect that the word is in fact spelt PGLOXQUY, the P being silent.

DOMINOES is a game for two people who have just found them after rummaging at the back of a drawer while every terrestrial and satellite channel is showing *It's A Wonderful Life* again.

The game starts when the first player says: "Have you ever played dominoes?" and the second replies: "No, but it's very simple, isn't it, don't you just sort of put the bits with corresponding blobs next to one another, and the one with most bits left over loses?"

The game goes on for a while until neither player has a bit that will lie next to anything. The first player then says: "There's got to be more to it than this," and the second player replies: "Well, you'd think so, wouldn't you?" The first player then goes off to try to find a book about dominoes, while the second player tries to stand the bits on top of one another. When the first player returns to say that for some reason there doesn't seem to be a book about dominoes in the house, the second player suggests that they see who can build the tallest pile of bits.

The game continues for about seven seconds, after which the players come to the conclusion that there is absolutely nothing wrong with watching *It's a Wonderful Life* for the fourteenth time.

The Grateful Dead

SINCE, once the coming Christmas is over, you will have to sit addle-brained among the yule detritus, struggling to compose thank-you letters, I thought I might kick-start you with a few inspirational examples from yesteryear...

Dear Uncle Fritz,
Thank you very much for the big round thing. I have not worked out how to play it yet because I cannot fit it under my chin and when I put it between my legs it

pops out again. I have tried sitting at it, but it rolls away, and when I blow it, it just gets bigger without any notes coming out. The boy next door says you kick it, but he is a fool, he is nearly six and still can't play the Toccata and Fugue. Maybe you pluck it.

Your devoted nephew,
Wolfgang Amadeus

Dear Mother,
Thank you for the slippers. They are good slippers. They have this thing the good slippers have, which is the woolly bobble on the top, and they have the fluffy stuff inside for when the cold comes down from the North.

But they also have this other thing which is not so good. It is the way it is with slippers, sometimes. It is where they are two sizes too big, and then what happens is they fall off, and this is a bad thing. It is one of the worst things there is. If you are running with the bulls and one of your slippers comes off, it can happen that you will end up with a wound Down There. With the big bulls of Pamplona it is good to have *afición*, and it is good to have *cojones*, but it is even better to have slippers that do not fall off.

When it is no longer Christmas and the yellow lights are on again in the stores, I shall do the thing where you go in and exchange them for mittens.

It will not be easy, but it must be done. That is the way it is.

Your loving son,
Ernest

Dear Daddy,

Thank you for the teddy bear and the stuffed donkey and the furry piglet and the stripy tiger. They are great fun for playing Big Game Hunter! I have hanged the teddy bear, and drowned the donkey (it was ever such fun in the bath tonight), and shoved a pointed stick up the pig's bum and roasted him over the nursery fire, and skinned the tiger and thrown his insides out of the window!

I asked Santa for a meat cleaver, but he did not bring it, so you probably won't have to advertise for another nanny for a bit.

Yours truly,
Christopher Robin

Cher Vincent,

Thank you so much for the ear. It was a most thoughtful gift, and I know just how much it must have meant to you to break up the set. Unfortunately, one of my other friends, an elegant gentleman from Béziers with several major retail outlets, was generous enough to send me a darling little poodle for Christmas; while I was decorating the tree, I carelessly left your ear in the bidet, and the dog got it.

How I wish things could have been otherwise; for example, if your ear had got the dog. But things do not always happen the way we want them to in this world, n'est-ce pas?

By the way, I am afraid I will not be able to see you again. I have never done it with a monaural person. and do not wish to start now. But that is just silly me being squeamish – I am sure you will find someone else.

Happy New Year!
Claudine Sauvignon

Dear Scott
Thank for the gloves. Smart, if a bit thin.

Oates

My dear Messrs Shadbolt and Truelove,
Words cannot express my gratitude for your munificent gift! I purchase my unguents and purgative jellies from your unparagoned emporium for their own excellent sake, and not in expectation of such egregious reciprocity. I see from the accompanying note that you live in hope of the continuance of my custom in 1660; well, gentlemen, you may rest assured upon that score!

The book is a veritable delight! I have long wanted a volume setting out the height of tides, phases of the moon, sedan rates, useful knots, foreign coinages, and so forth. That the bulk of the tome consists of blank pages is, I confess, something of a mystery to me, but I am certain that these will be put to good use, as pipe spills, ear reamers, laundry lists, or whatever.

Yours most gratefully,
Samuel Pepys

Flower Power

OH, look, there are millions and millions of them, beside the lake, beneath the trees, fluttering and dancing in the breeze. It is a nightmare. It is a scandal. It is a national tragedy. That is not where they should be, and it is not what they should be doing. They should be beside the petrol pumps, beneath the misplaced apostrophes, lying and wilting in the Cellophane: best daff's, 2 pounds' a bunch.

But they are not, they are still out there in the fields, tossing their heads in sprightly dance; and they will have to stay there, dancing ever less sprightlily (oh yes there is, look it up), until those heads rot off because there is nobody to cut them. One third of the daffodils in the country's main growing areas will go unharvested this year, we are told, thanks to a booming economy in which the traditional rural workforces have gone off to be Channel 5 presenters, chat-line sirens, Rolex fences etc, rather than break their backs for a fiver an hour, stretch'd in never-ending line along the margin of a bay. As the result of which the increasingly frantic industry is begging the Government to relax employment laws so that immigrants and asylum-seekers, legal and illegal both, can be drafted in to snip and wrap. They would be put up in top temporary accommodation, with roofs, fed and watered, and, I assume, be allowed to play the banjo in their own time.

Yes, exactly, that is why I so like this modest proposal, and why I think the Cabinet will, too: as a close observer of new Labour mission creep(s), I am struck by the thought that nothing could more pungently exude the whiff of Third Way than a Plantation Initiative: its humanitarian largesse towards all those poor sods legging it through the Chunnel would pull in socialist dissenters (I might call the policy a Short left hook, if I did puns), while keeping them under close observation and strict control would offer the macho Right a security, er, Blunkett.

Currently terror-stricken town-dwellers would unanimously applaud the sudden disappearance from their threatening streets of thousands of the desperate broke armed with everything from squeegees to Uzis, while countryfolk still bleeding from the twin barrels of foot-and-mouth and hunt-banning would leap at the chance both of converting their desolated landscapes into floral factories – fortuitously also putting the roses back into the tear-stained cheeks of lepidopterists, twitchers, ramblers, and all the other millions of ecologically challenged people in big boots – and of once again seducing to this blessed plot jumboloads of disaffected American tourists with the offer of a thousand opportunities to stay in an authentic antebellum theme park, sipping mint juleps on the verandah and cocking a nostalgic ear as the long summertime shadows fall across the flower pickers homeward plodding their weary way and lowing a selection of Stephen Foster favourites with all the natural rhythm for which the Balkan glottis is justly renowned.

Not to mention the occasional boon of a hue and cry, as someone decides he's had enough of homeward plodding and instead takes it on the lam in a bid for freedom, only to be pursued by the Quorn or the Belvoir or whichever other pack is locally handy, on the wholly legitimate grounds that a runaway slave is not a fox, and may therefore be hunted with impunity both from the Home Office and from animal rights saboteurs unmoved by quarry on only two legs. Foreign tourists would love all that: it's a hell of a lot more videogenic than filming Mrs Hackenplotz Jr teetering on her Manilo Blahniks to and fro across the Abbey Road zebra.

And wouldn't plantations also have an irresistible appeal to the hordes of footballers, pop idols, catwalkers, dot-com tycoons, soap stars, lottery winners and all the rest of the cash-heavy who currently constitute 60 per cent of the landed gentry because there is no other way of getting rid of the stuff? They buy great estates of ten thousand acres with no idea what to do there, except fall off their brand-new hunter, riddle three toes with their brand-new Purdey, or lose an eye to a cack-handed cast with their brand-new Sage, after which they want nothing to do with the countryside ever again and nor do their maimed weekending mates. But if they had a plantation, broad sunlit uplands of marijuana and poppy and coca, magic liberty caps snuggling among the oak roots, to be harvested and refined by slaves forced to keep their traps shut on pain of being summarily repatriated to Iraq? Would this not stay their disillusioned flight to Mustique bolt-holes and thus save the stately homes of England from terminal neglect?

I think so. I think the daffodils are trying to tell us something. This year dancing in the breeze, next year gone with the wind.

You Called Me Baby Doll A Year Ago

ONCE upon a time, like many a young shaver, I had a penchant for the older woman. It was as literal a penchant as any etymologist could shake a stick at: the instant the older woman appeared, my body would hinge suddenly upright in its seat and lean so far forward so incautiously that my chin would not come to rest until it had struck the seat in front; where it would remain, often for hours, while the older woman did her stuff. Thus, though I was so young a shaver that no blade had yet touched that chin, for most of my puberty it remained as rawly red as if I had taken it for its daily toilette to a local stonemason. The seats had sharp edges at the Barnet Odeon, in 1951.

Which was the year I fell for my first older woman. I was 13, Elizabeth Taylor was 18, and the film was *A Place in The Sun*, in which the most beautiful girl in the world did that kiss. You all know that kiss: it wasn't really a kiss at all, it was Montgomery Clift getting his face eaten, and

George Stevens shot it with so many cameras from so many angles that the Academy was left with no other option but to give him an Oscar for Best Kiss, since, had it not, ten million men would have stormed its ramparts and beaten the academicians to death with their own statuettes.

It took six months to get Liz's embouchure out of my dreams and it was only the bosom of my second older woman that finally replaced it, which was a bit unfair on my first older woman, because in a fantasy contest between a mouth and a bust, a bust will always win, hands down. There being, sadly, no other place for hands when you are a small 13 and Joan Collins is a big 18, as she was in *Cosh Boy*, a British bummer so witless as to be not so much a turkey as a drumstick. I shall, however, always remember it as a truly remarkable feature film, in that it contained a truly remarkable feature, cantilevered to so rigid a horizontality that I could have stood my entire collection of William books on it. More yet, it made a major contribution to my cultural development, too: that week, Form 3 was being introduced to the Romantics, who were leaving me pretty cold until we hit the line "Behold her bosom and half her side, a sight to dream of, not to tell!" and suddenly I saw that Sam Coleridge was somebody I could do business with.

It took a full year to wean me, if she will pardon the expression, off Miss Collins, and it also took Debbie Reynolds. Debbie, of course, was not a lust object, but I was a mature 14 by the time *Singin' In The Rain* came out and thus ready for a more meaningful relationship. Debbie was somebody you fell in love with. Debbie was the girl next door. Or, in my case, the older woman next door, and then only if you lived next door to the Barnet Odeon, but we had a wonderful time together, even in close-up, where her head was larger than our house. When Debbie parted those huge but still delectable lips to sing *You Were Meant For Me*, I knew that I was the you she meant.

And everything was wonderful, until, in 1954, VistaVision came along. Because VistaVision, which made everything even bigger, brought with it a musical called *Artists and Models*, and one of the models was, at 19, four years older than I. Now, even before VistaVision, Shirley MacLaine had the longest legs in the world, but VistaVision transformed her into one of that world's seven wonders: I walked into the cinema one afternoon, and there she was, the Colossus of Barnet. Two years had passed, Form 3 had become Form 5, we had done Shelley by then, so I knew there was always the risk that Shirley's legs might end up like Ozymandias's, but there was time enough for that. For now, I looked on Shirley's works and I went nuts.

But it is another now, now, which is why I am telling you all this. For, half a century on, these four older women who cornerstoned my puberty have convened – or, if you are me, conspired – for the first time, to make a movie together. It is called *These Old Broads*, it came out in the United States last week, it will appear over here any minute now, and it is thus about to be the worst thing that has happened to me since O level. Don't ask me why, ask the promotional publicity which sits before me as I type, and which, if my tear-dimmed eyes permit, I shall quote: *"These Old Broads* is a hilarious satire in which four of our most glamorous movie stars send their fabled screen images up rotten!" Rotten is right. I am in – let me quickly tot it up – Form 52 now, and just look, old broads, I have got as far as Yeats. I am reciting: "I have spread my dreams under your feet. Tread softly, because you tread on my dreams." But, as with so much else, it's a little late for that, now.

Amphibious Mission

NOTWITHSTANDING the fact that there are some six billion people on this planet, you would be pushed to find any two who had less in common than John Prescott and I. Stranded in a jammed lift with, say, a Dayak headhunter or an Uzbekhi stonemason, I feel confident we should be able to drum up some convivial topic to while away the jittery wait; but confine me there with the great Deputy and I rather fear there would be no sound but cleared throats, sucked teeth, and the intermittent click of a nibbled fingernail.

At least, I did rather fear that until an hour ago; when I suddenly learnt that not only did Mr Prescott have something in common with me, he also, even more remarkably, had something in common with Mayor Livingstone. A concern for newts. I know this, because my bathside radio told me so: a little after 8 o'clock, a murmur in my soapy ear identified itself as a spokesvoice for the

Department of the Environrnent and launched into a heart-rending plea for the common newt, for the unhappy reason that it is growing less common by the minute. Though this is the time when they seek to become more common by waking from hibernation and rushing off to mate, April is turning into an annually crueller month for the titchy amphibia: distanced ever further from our diminishing wetlands, they regularly conk out before meeting the newt of their dreams, so John's caring department is urging us to do all we can to help, by keeping an eye out for the knackered, gently scooping them up, and resettling them in the nearest pond.

You have to warm to a man like that, if you're me. I wonder, since he is but three weeks older than I, whether his attraction to the newt began with mine, 50 years back, he in Ellesmere Port, I in East Barnet, but each toddling home with a similar jam-jar. There was a small pond at the top of our road dug by a Focke-Wulf, which, since 1941, annually retained its winter water until well into June. It teemed with old Bournvita tins, bedsprings, ruined buckets, sexual detritus, handlebars, boots, fag packets, lavatory pans and, in April, newts. Where they came from to this aquatic slum I never knew, but one glance told me why: their hysterically tenacious drive to copulate despite the most unpropitious of circumstances was something I was not to encounter again until 20 years brought me to my first Fleet Street Christmas party.

I learnt a lot about newts back then. Decanted from jar to tank, they dined at depth, chomping on worms so long and energetic that a newt might sit for hours with one end of its lunch poking out of its mouth and the other end making its little spotty belly ripple with the unmistakable frenzy of a main course recognising that the writing was on the wall. They also mated with exemplary passion, the male grasping the female and hanging on all day, which was probably why timorous parents preferred to talk about birds and bees, who get it all over in half a second, usually in mid-air and not even noticing. I do not have the statistics to hand, but it is a fair bet that the work of the divorce courts could be drastically reduced if more people were brought up on newts.

Particularly since there is no truth in the foul canard that attaches to the newt's supposed drinking habits: I have observed newts for 50 years, man and boy, and have never seen them touch the stuff. Sober as a judge, is what newts are; indeed, since I have also observed judges for 50 years, man and boy, it is my considered opinion that the two popular similes have in fact become mixed up.

I also discovered that the newt was not a newt at all, but an ewt, a Middle English variant of *eft*, a sequence of nom-de-plumage so fraught with philological conundra that, if you mention it to an academic linguist, he will begin jumping up and down and dragging enough books from his shelves to fuel a Nazi barbecue; because it all starts with the Old English *eveta*, whose origin dictionaries prefer to leave unknown, despite the obvious fact that it must refer to some lost Anglo-Saxon musical about an ambitious, and possibly amphibian, woman. Grendel's mother, perhaps.

None of this, I'm sure, will come as any surprise to John: he cares, therefore he knows. Even now, I suspect, he is driving slowly up and down some riparian street with the radiant Pauline hanging out of the Jag window, careless of her coiffe, scanning for footsore newts. How very reassuring it is to have at least one member of the Government who not only has some affinity with threatened animals, but is also swift to act! Come the next election, John shall not find me wanting.

Stands England Where It Did?

WERE you an asylum-seeker, bogus or not, adrift in London with nothing to keep body and soul together but a few lurid facts about how long it took Sir Albert Hall to build The Bloody Abbey (where Winston the Ripper strangled the two little ponces), then the name of Mr Guy Merrick should so strike terror into your heart as to have you immediately hurtling round to Jack Straw's side entrance on bended knees, begging for a repatriation chitty to get you back home on the morning tide. Because Mr Merrick is a senior banana at the Association of London Tour Guides, and he has just this minute been on my radio to make my flesh creep about the imminent spring.

For it is also, of course, the imminent tourist season, and what is agitating Mr Merrick is the fact that London is teeming with amateur guides, mainly ex-Balkan, who are grabbing tourists at their assorted disembarkation points and filling their heads with a load of old codswallop at throwaway prices which not only terminally undercut the impeccably informed professionals, but also pose a threat, says Mr Merrick, to all we have and are. Or, more accurately, to all we had and were: because the unscrupulous Kosovan wildcatters know only marginally more about the subject under guidance than their illicitly buttonholed listeners, with the result that satisfied customers from Osaka and Wagga Wagga and Moose Nuts, Wyoming, are returning home under the impression that the Post Office Tower was built by Edward XII for Lily Langtry, the inventor of the jersey, and that the Monument in Trafalgar Square to commemorate the Great Fire of 1588 is topped by a statue of Oliver Cromwell, who started it. None of this, of course, would probably matter very much were it not for the fact that when the home movies begin flickering in the wide-screened parlours of Moose Nuts and the proud host begins reeling off the, to him, relevant data, someone in the audience who made the trip a month earlier is going to leap to his feet and ask what Oliver Cromwell – the brilliant librettist who, with Sir Stanley Laurel, wrote *HMS Mikado* – is doing on top of a column put up by Henry VIII in honour of his marriage to Anne Hathaway. Out of the ensuing mêlée, Mr Merrick warns us, England is going to emerge in very bad odour since nobody likes to blow ten thousand bucks in return for a mile of humiliatingly inaccurate videotape.

Worse still, the deception is not being confined to the metropolis but is spreading pestilentially to every touristic corner of the queendom, like Stratford and Canterbury and Bath and Edinburgh, as gullible travellers are being hustled aboard unscrupulous, not to say unroadworthy, minibuses and shipped off to see the birthplace of Sir Walter Byron, the Old Pretender, or the parsonage where the Beverley Sisters wrote *Vanity Heights*. No doubt some of them aren't even being taken to the famous destination specified, but being dropped instead at Croydon and llford, pointed at the nearest photogenically derelict sink-estate, and given a lecture in Serbian undertone about Stonehenge, that ancient temple where descendants of the original Androids still congregate to perform their arcane ceremonies, every Guy Fawkes Night.

And as if even all this were not enough, Mr Merrick also warns us of bogus tourist souvenirs which these shameless charlatans are apparently cobbling together in covert sweatshops and passing off as the genuine article. He did not specify any typical examples, but one can easily imagine, can one not, a scale model of Queen Victoria, dressed as a Beefeater, who plays *It's A Long Way to Tipperary* when her hat is lifted, carrying an ashtray in the shape of King Charles's severed head and a miniature of Blackpool Tower to which is attached a tiny tea-towel showing the Beatles signing Magna Carta.

So then, just how much should any of this worry us? Quite a lot, if Mr Merrick's preferred solution finds favour with Ken Livingstone: he wants the mayor to infiltrate his fiefdom with coppers disguised as well-heeled foreign visitors, who will entrap the fake guides and drag them off to the nearest beak to be charged with fraud. This is really bad news for Londoners like me: waylaid by a bewildered tourist, I generally try to do the best I can, despite my skimpy metropolitan knowledge. So, should the kindness of your heart betray you, too, into doing the same, and should you one day soon find yourself approached on the steps of St Paul's by a camera-hung man in jellaba and a stetson and handmade Italian loafers, who points up at the dome and says, "'Allo, 'allo, 'allo, mon ami, what's all this, then?" – mind how you go.

Taking A Chance On Love

I received the card yesterday. It is on my desk as I write. It is a big card, with a plump pink satin heart on the cover. Beneath the heart, in flowery script, runs the message: "Dearest Valentine, keep this heart away from children: although it is made from environmentally benign biodegradable material, a child could eat it and choke. When you have read the text inside, please destroy the card by taking it to an authorised municipal dump. Do not attempt to burn it or cut it up, fires can easily spread and 13 per cent of all domestic accidents involve scissors or other sharp instruments. We have sent you this card because we love you; that is also why we have signed it, because research shows that receiving an unsigned card may cause stress and anxiety, leading, in some cases, to stroke or cardiac infarct, possibly both. Warning: when you open the card, take great care not to cut your finger on the edge, this could eventuate septicaemia, which if not treated in time might involve amputation. From your loving Health & Safety Executive." You will not have received a card like mine, unless you, too, work in the communications industry. When I finally – and, of course, cautiously – opened the card, the first sentence I read explained that, as a leading opinion-former, I had been chosen to pass on essential precautionary Valentine information to my readers, to minimise the risk of their doing themselves a mischief. Here, therefore, are the other sentences.

☐ **Flowers:** Do not send flowers to a loved one. She may suffer from a floral allergy. Even if not, she could prick herself on a thorn, or get stung by something lurking inside the flower. If you are sent flowers and are prepared to accept them despite the risks, ask the delivery person to give the bunch a good shake before handing them over. But not before you have asked the deliverer to prove his identity: on Valentine's Day, criminals may avail themselves of the floral opportunity to burst into your house and maim or kill you, before stealing everything you have. When putting the flowers in a vase, be sure to turn off the tap: domestic drowning is on the increase. NB: Though your caring HSE is, of course, non-genderist, we are assuming that only women will be sent flowers, since common sense dictates that sending flowers to a man is really risky: it could trigger either orientation-doubt or perception-fear, each of which could terminally destabilise him.

☐ **Champagne:** To be avoided at all costs. Most ocular accidents are caused by champagne corks, the popping of which can also traumatise pets. Chilled drenching can lead to bronchitis, and in many inner-city areas, a loud bang may precipitate an exchange of gunfire. If you do insist on opening a bottle, do not drink it: 12 per cent of all domestic accidents involve walking into the furniture or falling downstairs.

☐ **Chocolates:** Never give chocolates. Caffeine accelerates the heart-rate, fats increase cholesterol, sugar creates obesity, and Belgium causes 32 per cent of all British cavities. Once these have been filled, 78 per cent of them, asked to deal with a hazel-nut cluster, will then need to be filled again. Worse, coffee-creams, which nobody ever eats, may lie around for so long that the recipient forgets it is a coffee cream, a fact which emerges only at the post mortem.

☐ **Cuddly toys:** On Valentine's Day, thousands of unthinking lovers exchange furry animals. What they exchange them for is their health: 32 per cent of all undiagnosable diseases are found in patients who have gone to bed cuddling a thing consisting of an ersatz outside from Taiwan stuffed with an ersatz inside from Pyongyang. While almost anything can be caught off the outside, there is almost nothing that cannot be caught off the inside, especially after the outside comes unstitched in the middle of the night and the inside comes out. If you have to give your beloved an animal, make it a real live one: should he or she catch anything off it, a vet will at least have something to go on.

☐ **Candlelit dinners:** Are you serious? 93 per cent of all domestic conflagrations to which emergency services are called on February 14 are caused by dingbats leaning across a red-checked tablecloth to kiss one another, bringing two flaming Chianti bottles to the ground, where they rapidly roll towards the curtains. Should you be mad enough to go ahead with a meal like that anyway, for God's sake keep a case of champagne in the room. Not, of course, for drinking (see above), only for spraying on the flames while waiting for the fire brigade to arrive.

Aesop and After

ONCE upon a time, and an imminent time it was, a fox stood under a tree, gazing up at a pigeon, and the pigeon stood in the tree, gazing down at the fox. They had been standing there that way for some while, during which the fox had been trying desperately to persuade the pigeon to sing, by telling it what a really terrific voice it had. Whitney Houston is not in the same league, cried the fox: eat your heart out, Charlotte Church, cried the fox; don't give up the day job, Lesley Garrett, cried the fox; do you know who is turning in her grave, cried the fox, Ella Fitzgerald is turning in her grave!

Now, anyone who has ever heard a pigeon sing will at once perceive that the fox was lying in its teeth, and it was doing this because it wanted something else in its teeth. What it wanted was the piece of mouldy cheeseburger that the pigeon was holding in its beak, and it reasoned that if only it could persuade the pigeon to open its beak, then the piece of mouldy cheeseburger would drop and find its rightful place in the fox's teeth. The pigeon, however, was wise to this, because it had spent several happy hours in the Reading Room of the British Museum, snacking on tasty titbits of gum and half-morocco, and it thus knew its Aesop like the back of Horatio Nelson's hand. You may wonder – since you have not yet reached the imminent time when these events took place – how the pigeon managed to have the run of the Reading Room and why nobody shot it, chucked a book at it, or even gently shooed it away, because you do not know that, in the imminent time, pigeons had the run of everywhere. They had become not merely a protected species, but a cherished species, a worshipped species, not least because they had really smart lawyers who had argued this, and really smart legislators who had enacted this, so this was the way it was. What was smart about these men and women, of course, was that they had opted to support the pigeons rather than have their nice houses blown up or their nice kneecaps shot off by people who loved pigeons more than anything. When I tell you that it was they who chopped down Nelson's Column (demolishing, as it toppled, the National Gallery, and flattening several hundred Japanese photographers) to make more room for pigeons, you will see just how much they loved them.

Pigeons, mind, were no less beloved than foxes, because foxes had all those same friends in high places, too, enabling all the country's foxes gleefully to migrate to London (where the best food and accommodation were to be found) following enlightened legislation that gave foxes free rail-passes, made it an offence not to offer them lifts, and withdrew licences from any hotelier refusing overnight hospitality; which was partly why London's pigeons and foxes now outnumbered London's bipeds by about twenty to one. Only partly, because there were also far fewer human Londoners in the imminent time, thanks to millions of them having either dropped dead from things they had caught off the pigeons and the foxes, or fled the capital to avoid dropping dead, especially as, following further caring legislation, all the hospitals were now run by vets and treated only sick pigeons or foxes. And even if you were not ill or dead, there were countless other risks to be run by sharing London with pigeons and foxes: if, for example, you owned a car and flaunted your institutional pigeonism by attempting to clean droppings off it, thereby causing grave emotional distress to the feathered community, you incurred heavy fines and lost your licence immediately, and should you run over a fox, a prison sentence was mandatory. If it was on a fox crossing at the time, you got life.

Sadly, however, the conjoint metropolitan bliss of fox and pigeon could not last. As the human exodus inevitably progressed, and larders emptied, and super-markets closed, and restaurants went bust, pretty soon there was not enough food to go round, and what little there was – mainly from illicit hamburger-stands run by Balkan refugees, a stubborn and nerveless breed – was, as it was bound to be, disputed between the foxes and the pigeons. That was how the fox came to be standing under the tree; where it was just on the point of telling the pigeon standing in the tree that if only it would sing *Somewhere Over The Rainbow*, it could become the greatest gay icon of all time, when the pigeon fell out of the tree, right at the fox's feet. The cheeseburger, composed mainly of bovine spinal cord and listeria, had killed it. The fox, unfortunately not knowing this, gobbled the tempting nugget, and, a moment or two later, lay stone dead beside the pigeon. Whereupon silence, at last, descended upon Trafalgar Square.

Moral: Beware of the cow.

Hot Air

ONCE upon a time, that time being the crisp misty morning of December 17, 1962, I ran 50m in the impressive time of 12 seconds. What, you will inquire in a second or two of your own – after you have done the thing with the fingers and calculated that I was 24 at the time – is so impressive about that? It is well below the Junior Infants' three-legged record, giggling mothers have beaten that time in a sack, middle-aged fathers have done it while not only balancing an egg on a spoon but also dropping it a couple of times en route; why are you buttonholing us with this now, Christmas is coming, we have wrapping to do, we have cards to send, we have stuff to stuff, we have trees to stand back up, we have fairy-lights to shout at, why should we break off in the middle of all this while some old fool witters on about...

So I'll tell you. What was impressive about it was that I had covered the distance faster than the aeroplane that had covered it before me. Oh, sure, I could have run it much faster, being then as slim as a flute and not yet seriously embarked upon my smoking career, I could have run it at a speed which would have put the plane to shame, but I wasn't there to put the plane to shame, I was there to pay it homage. For the there was Kitty Hawk, North Carolina, and the date was precisely 59 years after Orville Wright had clambered aboard his motorised cat's cradle, taken it up, and 12 seconds and 50m later, brought it down again – a success far greater than even he could have guessed, given that he took off on time, was not required to divert himself to Gatwick, or struggle to unwrap an inflight meal less palatable than its packaging, or queue, biting his knuckle, for the lavatory, that he had enough leg-room to avoid a pulmonary embolism and enough fresh air to avoid legionnaire's disease, did not get his ear sheared off by a duty-free trolley or his conk punched for asking the party in the seats behind to do the hokey-cokey less noisily, and did not discover, upon landing, that his luggage had been sent to Oslo. That was why I ran the same distance in the same time. I was a sentimental kid, back then.

Which brings me, and you – if you would care to lay aside that hammer and mistletoe and pay attention – to back now, and more to the point, to the point. For it brings me to another crisp, misty, and momentous December 17, the one just gone, 97 years after Orville Wright's big day; it brings me to Richard Branson's big day, when Sunday's media reported that Virgin Atlantic had placed an order for six of the new A3XX Airbuses, which will be the biggest aircraft ever built and contain not only 1,000 passengers but also, according to Virgin's press release, "shops, gyms, bars, playrooms, and 40 cabins containing double beds". How wonderful, you will cry, but do you know how literally wonderful it was? Prepare to cry again, for the fact is that, according to the A3XX specifications carried by the papers, the new plane's cabin is 50m long. Now, though Orville couldn't fly the length of it in 12 seconds today, nor I run it, the pair of us being somewhat past our best, you have to admit that there is a lot of wonderful coincidence rattling around in all this; some of it, perhaps, just a mite ironic.

I cannot of course speak for the Wright brothers: though I see from their notebooks that their dream was "to mimic the birds", the copy I have was edited, in 1953, by A.W. MacFarlane, who may well, for reasons of space, have cut out the bit about their other dream being to mimic Brent Cross. I can, however, speak for myself: I really don't know how much I want to travel the world in the company of boozy thousands mooching through Tie Rack and Body Shop and Virgin Megastore, or pumping iron and hip-hopping aerobically in Lycra phalanx and karaoking on sunbeds, while their fellow-travellers, 80 at a time, join the Mile High Club, and their children hurtle shrieking round the go-kart circuit two floors down.

But then again, I really don't know how much I want to travel the world at all, now that what Orville started has more or less finished the world I used to want to travel. Indeed, it may well be that Sir Richard is even cannier than we have always taken him to be: I see from his press release that he hasn't yet decided whether his new megacraft will have GEC or Rolls-Royce engines, and it could be that he plans, when they are put into service in 2006 and travel has become, with every passing day, exponentially grislier than it is now, for them not to have any engines at all. Given that his passengers will be able to have exactly the holiday they want without ever leaving the ground, what point is there in taking off in the first place?

I wish I could ask the man who did.

Unbeaten Tracks

Last Sunday, as a pigtailed Judy Garland spiralled past your windows and the mackerel struck out across your lawns and your bobbing cars resonated and morphed to the syncopated thrummings of the Hailstone Steel Band, many of you will, I know, have reacted by pulling tight the curtains and snuggling deep into your nest of travel supplements in the hope of palliating the present misery by laying plans for future escape. To, of course, some blissfully undiscovered spot.

And I know just as surely that you will have crawled out again, some hours later, less blissful than ever. For you will have discovered only that there is nowhere left undiscovered; that there is nowhere to escape to, because everyone has escaped there already. There is no desert island where ten thousand packagees are not stretched out on the sand like serried biltong, no rainforest where the plump drops no longer hit the ground, thanks to the impenetrable testudo of ten thousand brim-to-brim panamas trooping off behind their guide to video some parakeet or other, no dune unbuggied, no reef unscubaed, no souk unhaggled. Survey mankind from China to Peru, everyone accepts plastic.

But you are wrong. It is not so. For I, too, spent Sunday scouring all the holiday columns, not for countries that were listed, but for those that were not. And on Monday, just for you, I did a little research into what are clearly spots hitherto unspoilt, so that you, if you are quick, can be the lucky ones to spoil them first. It is not, of course, a complete list, I am not a chump, a complete list is available only for a used tenner and an sae to Robson Books (mark the envelope Coren Pension Fund), but it is at least a taster, to get you, in every sense, going. Let us start with the Ellice Islands. These were formerly the Gilbert & Ellice Islands until the Act of Severance of October 1975. In the Ellice Islands the natives speak Ellice, but you can get by on a smattering of Gilbert (Ruddigore always goes down well with waiters). They are made up of nine small islands, Nanumea, Nanamunga, Niutao, Nui, Vaitupu, Nukufetau, Nukulaelae, Nurakita, and Funafutu. Nukulaelae is probably the least uninteresting, and you will therefore want to know the quickest method of getting there: your best course is to travel to Funafutu, somehow, and see if anyone's going that way.

If you prefer islands closer to home, the Juan

Fernandez group, some 500 miles off Chile, are justly famous for their eating. The inhabitants will eat anything. Your best course would be to coat your luggage with alum. Do not send clothes away for dry cleaning, do not leave shoes outside your door at night, and carry your golf clubs at all times. Evening is the time to watch the fairly famous Tordillo, a form of bowls played with glass eyes.

A far more accessible insular spot I spotted for being so far unspotted is Bornholm, a small island on the Baltic Riviera best known for being the home of Bornholm's Disease, a highly contagious viral infection. In summer, Bornholm is staggeringly cheap and unaccountably empty, and thus indistinguishable from the way it is in winter. The few locals you might spot are immensely friendly, but it is usually possible to get away from them by running, since the majority are attached to saline drips. The island's principal souvenir is rectal thermometers.

Baffin Bay, too, went entirely unmentioned in the travel sections, despite its wonderful beach. You have to dig a while to find it,mind, but if you go 50 or 60ft down below the summer ice-cap, you will catch that rare sight, topless Eskimos. They are, you will soon find, much like holidaymakers anywhere else, although they have never discovered the deckchair: if an Inuit wants to get his fingers caught in something, he uses a bear-trap. They have, however, developed a form of French cricket, using a seal. The ice-cream is warm, but not wholly unpleasant, and a small bottle of zero-factor sunbloc will usually suffice for a fortnight.

Travellers in search of quiet, out-of-the-way Eurasian resorts might find just what they want in Kazakhstan. As its name implies, Kazakhstan has no pier to speak of, but there is an amusement arcade in Frunze, at the foot of the Tsien Shan, which gives good change. The best time to go is early August when, as the result of inordinately high temperatures, dead fish float to the surface of the Aral Sea. They are not edible, but huge crowds come down to the foreshore to watch the fish bump into one another, and many a cheery Kazakh will be only too happy to share his tzarnishdi with a hungry foreigner. It is a bicycle made from war-surplus guttering.

Wise Moves

MY heart aches, and a drowsy numbness pains my sense, which is a bit unusual for me in that it is normally brought on by nightingales, not owls: But when, on Monday morning, my newspaper announced, from its position against the Kelloggs carton, that the Prime Minister was having a bird-box installed at Chequers so that he and his family could watch another family doing what comes naturally, my head suddenly swam so unsettlingly that my first thought was to check the carton's ingredients list in case this was New Enriched Kelloggs With Added Hemlock.

But no: a moment's reflective reeling reassured me that what had so staggered me was merely Mr Blair's insouciance. This bird-box could do for him. This bird-box is an election-box: what is inside the former may well determine what, in a few years' time, goes inside the latter. Because what is inside the former is a family of owls, and owls being the nocturnal items they are, this is no ordinary box: the bird-fancier does not watch the residents popping in and out, he watches them staying in, and he can do this only because this is a high-tech box, fitted with an infra-red camera for night-watching which beams its pictures to a television set. What we are talking here is Peeping Tony.

More of this later. First, how did he get the box? He did not buy it with his own money, he did not even touch Geoffrey Robinson for a loan; this box was that most political of chalices, a gift. There is no such thing as a free bird-box. Even if the donor has attached no strings to the box, even if he is grinding no axe for Tony's neck, there are umpteen action groups, tabloid hacks and political enemies frothing to do the business, viz, why is the PM so interested in putting roofs over feathered heads when human homeless kip on doorsteps? Why is a rurally illiterate townie interfering in the natural ways of owls, whom God intended in his infinite wisdom to enter trees through holes, not bungalows through doors? Why is he so ignorantly keen to nurture predators who are wiping out our little voles? And if he's suddenly so interested in the countryside, wouldn't he be better off spending his evenings grappling with genetic modification, river pollution, vanishing bus routes/sub post-offices/village schools/banks/doctors, greenfield despoliation, post-fox job losses, lamb prices, fuel prices, flood-barriers, instead of sitting there watching owls hop about on the telly?

157

With his wife. Bad enough she is out there all day in one of her 400 different couturier numbers earning a million a year instead of seeing there is a hot meal on the table, without coming in and plumping herself down in front of the box when she ought to be sewing name-tags on to the tutus and polo jodhpurs of her selectively educated kids. And while we're on the subject, what is she wearing tonight, could it be a special owl-watching peignoir run up just for her by Versace, with matching Manolo Blahnik maribou-trimmed mules? Or possibly mule-trimmed maribous, she does not give a toss about our dumb friends, she cares only about *their* dumb friends, hallo Salman, hallo Elton, hallo Damien, why not come over for a magnum or two, cook is doing a sucking-pig, we're all watching owls, such fun!

And what are they watching the owls doing? Exactly. If Lord Holme had been caught watching that, he wouldn't have lasted five minutes at the Broadcasting Standards Commission, never mind a year. And while we're on the subject, why does the PM have his own little owl channel, why can't we all have that, aren't these People's Owls, or what?

And what about owl abuse? Owls have rights, I bet if you look in that new Human Rights wossname there is stuff about entitlement to privacy of all feathered Europeans, course his wife'd get him off, they would probably fix the jury, don't talk to me about cronyism, I had that Derry Wallpaper in the back of the cab once...

And then, as suddenly as it had descended, the drowsy numbness lifted, and I saw clearly, for the first time, what the Prime Minister might have been up to in accepting the gift, despite its inherent risks.

For is there not something of Christopher Robin about our great leader? Coming downstairs, holding his beloved Gordon-the-Pooh by the foot, bumpety-bump, off to the wood to meet Eeyore Prescott and Tigger Cook, and Piglet Straw, and Baroness Kanga, and Rabbit Mandelson and all Rabbit's friends and relations... but which stuffed animal has never numbered among his playmates, and what property has the happy band of chums thus always lacked? Yes, of course, you are ahead of me. They have never had anyone wise. They have never, up until now, had Owl.

Small Farmer

ON Christmas Day 1950, dawn found me, because it knew exactly where to look, springing from my little bed, with my little heart going pit-a-pat, and hurtling downstairs on my little feet, because I also knew exactly where to look. It would be beside the living-room fireplace: a big holly-papered box, with a fort inside it. I didn't need to take the paper off to know there was a fort inside it, because I had been dropping heavy hints since early October, hints so daily elaborated that I knew that when I did take the paper off I would find not only a turreted pile with a working drawbridge, but also phalanxes of lead infantrymen with titchy sword-arms you could make go up and down, and ranks of lead cavalry with bandy legs you could make get on and off their horses, and a field-gun you could fire matches out of, and wagons, and pennants, and a boat for the moat.

So you will appreciate that it was with something of a shock to my little system when I did rip the holly-paper off to find a box containing none of these. What it contained was a barn and a silo and a cart and a tractor and phalanxes of lead yokels with titchy scythe-arms you couldn't be bothered to make go up and down, and ranks of lead pigs and cows and chickens and sheep and horses with nobody bandy on them at all. And little stooks and churns. And a little dog. And nothing that fired match-sticks. I looked at all this for a long time, wondering what had gone wrong: had my father been slowly going deaf (he had had a noisy war) so that all the hints had fallen on ears no longer competent at distinguishing between fort and farm? Had my mother been slowly going pacifist (she had had a melancholy war) so that distaffs had prevailed over pike staffs? I didn't know then and hadn't the heart to ask, so I don't know now. I know only that I never much fancied the countryside after that. And worse was to come, a little later.

But a little earlier than that little later, my chagrin was slightly palliated when David Bunyan came over to play with the new fort I'd told him I was getting and brought his new howitzer, which fired ballbearings. He took one look at my new farm (my father had suggested pillows for hills, which were now dotted with little animals) and being an inventive child, immediately declared that the yokels were British, the pigs Germans, the sheep Americans, the horses Russians, the chickens Italians, and the little dog was Hitler, and the tractor was a tank and the cart was a Bren-gun carrier, so we plotted tactics and sent them into mortal combat, and the yokels blew the pigs off the silo with the howitzer while the sheep drove the chickens out of the barn so that the horses (sworn to take no prisoners) could wipe them out to a chicken, and the game ended when the little dog shot himself, and it was a pretty good game, all in all. But I never played with the farm again. It just stayed set up in my room, exemplar of that bogus bucolic idyll which so many Englishmen hold so dear, gathering dust.

Which brings me, or did in a very short while, to the worse which was to come, when, as 1951 broke, *The Archers* stormed the BBC and did away with *Dick Barton*. And what was Brookfield but my toy farm to the life? Or, at least, to the Sound Effects department: where once our wireless had rocked to the thwack of uppercut and the crack of Webley, now cows went moo and sheep went baa and chickens went cluck, and yokels went oh, ah, me old love, me old beauty, and every night this pabulum fed the English pastoral fancy. Until, as it was bound to do, a tooth bit into the Ambridge apple, and sin entered the garden of England, and *The Archers* came to seethe with lust and crime and greed and drugs, and all the bad stuff of the world outside, and the English no longer had a rural dream to dream, and wept for the Ambridge of yesteryear.

Which is a great pity, because there is real money in it. That occurred to me this morning, while I was in the loft of my new house sorting the detritus of my old house while my trannie rabbited on about both *The Archers* jubilee and the future of the Dome, and there it suddenly was, my old farm, jumbled in its old box, and I thought Yes! (I may have punched the air) because suppose some spry entrepreneur were to reconstruct the original, unspoilt innocent Ambridge within the Dome, green hills dotted with free-range stock, lanes a-stroll with virgin milkmaids and tongue-tied grooms, the Bull a smoky place of pickled eggs and lukewarm bitter, meadows of buttercups and hedge-rows of unofficial roses, if our Kublai Khan were to decree all that, would not, at last, and just in the nick of time, the world beat a path to his door? Especially if there were something steaming on the path, and the door creaked.

Arts Counsel

Today's bumless seats presage tomorrow's cashless coffers, and the arts are in a predictable tizz about how, if audiences and money don't start coming in soon, they will cope. Well, my arts counsel is to nip and tuck...

Dear Diary:
Tuesday: Absolutely splendid performance by Simon Rattle at the Royal Festival Hall last night! Despite a biting gale blowing off the Thames, Sir Simon managed to bring his knees together with remarkable elan for the cymbal parts, and his harmonica solos suffered hardly at all from the demands made by the drum on his back and

the spoons in his frostbitten fingers. It may not, of course, have been everyone's idea of the Choral Symphony, but given that the cash-strapped RFH had perforce been hired out to ITV for a gala performance of *Who Wants To Be A Millionaire?*, all congratulations must surely be proffered to Sir Simon for his exemplary courage and commitment.

NB: Sadly, Nicholas Hytner was unlucky enough to be knocked out in the first round of the quiz and consequently went home with nothing; which sadly means that the National Theatre's eagerly anticipated major production of *Antony and Cleopatra* will now be performed by glove puppets.

Wednesday: Looked in at the Royal Opera House last evening for the final dress rehearsal of *Il Trovatore*, and cannot help feeling that its tragic grandeur is somewhat diminished by being sung on stilts. This is due to the fact that while *Il Trovatore* is being performed 10ft above the stage, the other half of the Verdi Festival, *Rigoletto*, is simultaneously being performed beneath. While this enables the ROH to be used on alternate evenings as a bingo hall, thus subsidising its musical ventures, it does lead to unfortunate confusion not only in the audience, but also among the company: yesterday, for example, Gilda flung out an incautious arm during her Act 1, Scene ii, aria, and struck the stilt of Manfrico in the opera above, toppling him into a kettledrum. I was, however, delighted to learn later in the day that Signor Pavarotti is coming along nicely in Bart's intensive care unit, and expects to be back calling the bingo by the end of the month, and singing again early in the new year.

Thursday: It is rare indeed for a theatre buff to find himself watching the definitive *King Lear*, and it is therefore particularly distressing to record, dear Diary, that what promised to be an exceptionally sensitive, intelligent, and moving interpretation of the play by the Royal Shakespeare Company at the Aldwych last night should have been marred immediately after the First Act interval, when the scene suddenly changed to the Kowalski scullery in New Orleans. Now, I am as devoted an enthusiast of Tennessee Williams as any man, but even I am compelled to observe that the master's *chef d'oeuvre* loses something of its intended impact when sandwiched between the Fool's closing obscene couplet and, a scant scene later, the unsettling appearance of Hedda Gabler at, I believe, Toad Hall – especially after Blanche Dubois's major, and seminal, soliloquy was forced to compete with the pas de deux from *Don Quixote* being performed simultaneously on top of the Kowalski fridge by a pair of temperamental Russian dancers recently evicted from the Albert Hall for refusing to pirouette for the crowd's diversion between rounds five and six of the European Middleweight Championship: a singular piece of selfish foolhardiness, in my view, given the cost of tutus and the legendary generosity of boxing fans prepared to throw even folding money into the ring when entertained by someone willing to have a bit of a go.

Friday: Bewildering news reaches me from Tate Britain. Expecting the usual hordes of visitors to the exhibition of contenders for the Turner Prize, the gallery was stunned this morning when only one turned up, a Mr Geoff Pierce of Palmers Green. Not only did he refuse to buy a catalogue, a toasted tea-cake, a cup of coffee, a calendar, or even a picture postcard of *The Fighting Temeraire Entering Harbour*, he took from beneath his raincoat a felt-tipped pen and a piece of cardboard on which he wrote Silly Arse Who Only Came In To Get Out Of The Rain And Was Forced To Spend Two Hours Looking At A Load Of Crap, My Cat Could Do Better, and hung it around his neck. He then entered himself for the prize. An authoritative source at William Hill informs me that, in a further devastating blow to our already beleaguered culture, Mr Pierce is now the 11-2 on favourite to win.

Fear of Flying

IT being May 8, and thus the 57th anniversary of VE-Day, may I take this opportunity to wish all my readers many happy no returns? Especially as these are unsettlingly evocative eurotimes not only generally, but also particularly, given that Jack Straw has chosen this resonant moment to fly to America on a bond-strength-ening mission, and we are all therefore feeling both a little trepidant and a little bereft, since Britain without Jack Straw is like Hamlet without Polonius. And you may have been shaken, too, to read, on the very same day, that Lufthansa had pressed a refurbished wartime Junkers Ju52 into service to fly nostalgic trips over

London. However, I am assured by its press office that nostalgia will be allowed to go only so far, and you in your turn should be assured by recent memorial events which showed that we still have two Spitfires and a Lancaster, and Lufthansa would therefore be ill-advised to try anything funny (despite the legendary German sense of humour, I might add, but only because Iain Duncan Smith is in no position to sack me).

In fact, I myself am pretty nostalgic about the Ju52. You could tell just how nostalgic if you were sitting here beside me, because on my desk I have, as a paperweight, a fist-sized chunk of jagged steel. It wasn't always a paperweight, mind; it started life – and did its best, indeed, to finish it – as part of a bomb that blew down my grandfather's greenhouse in 1942. If I touch it now, it is as with Proust sinking a delicate incisor into his madeleine: *The Night the Fairey Aviation Works at Hayes Copped It* leaps intact from the pop-up book of infant memory with all its sense-data intact. I can hear the greenhouse at 4 Copeland Avenue collapse. I can smell the dust from the carpet inside the Morrison shelter in the dining-room being beaten into my nostrils by the concussions half a mile away. I can see the lurching shadows on the dining-room wall projected by the orange glow flaring up when my grandfather tore open the blackout curtains to see what the crash was all about, and hear him shouting, "They've got the greenhouse! They've got the greenhouse!", as if it had been the Luftwaffe's chief priority, Junkers pilots four miles up cheering and congratulating one another on having at last wiped out the tomatoes at 4 Copeland Avenue, breaking radio silence to inform an ecstatic Goering, leaning out into the chill blackness to paint yet another greenhouse on the fuselage, and, at last, turning joyously for home, arms linked, singing – having proved that they were – fit to bust.

And this is the piece of shrapnel that did it. I went out into the garden the next morning with my grandfather, who had painted DIG HERE FOR DAVE on the tin ARP helmet he always wore outdoors in case he was buried by rubble, and I picked up the piece of shrapnel, and, a long lifetime on, I can still recall not only that it felt warm, but exactly how warm.

And it was because of May 8 that it is the only piece of shrapnel I have: at the Osidge School VE-Day party, I swapped the rest of my collection with Gerald Finch, who was sitting next to me, in exchange for his signed letter from the King, thanking all children for helping him to win the war. I am looking at it now, and 57 years on I still feel uneasy about it, because, although there is no name on it to blow the gaff to posterity, it is not my letter. It is Gerald Finch's letter. As a matter of fact, I am curiously relieved to get that off my chest; it has been something of a burden, all these years. It isn't that, six decades ago, I received no gratitude from George VI. It was there, beside the commemorative mug and the titchy Union Flag, when I sat down at the trestle table in the playground. I read it, and I looked at the signature, and Dorothy Pickering opposite said I bet he didn't sign every one, I bet that's not real ink, I bet it's printed, and I said I bet it isn't, I bet it's real, and I licked my finger and I rubbed the signature, and it wasn't real, and Dorothy Pickering said you should've washed, it's got a big dirty smear on it now, you can't frame that, so I got my handkerchief out and tried to rub the dirt off and the print started coming away, and Gerald Finch said now you've done it, I bet you can go to prison for mucking up a King's letter. Then he offered to let me have his, in return for my shrapnel collection.

I wonder what happened to Gerald Finch. Probably a billionaire by now.

So what is the upshot of all this? Yes, spot on, I shall be popping down, come July, to City Airport built on the fortuitously flattened East End, for it is from there that the Ju52 will be taking off down memory lane. I'll take my shrapnel. We're chums, now, you know. And it's not as if the lights are going out all over Europe, is it? They're only starting to flicker a bit.

Naked Truth

I AM inside now, typing. But up until a few minutes ago, I was outside, worrying. I was standing on my front step and staring out across the little octagon of greensward which separates the three houses on my side from the three houses opposite. And I was not standing alone. There was a ghost standing beside me, in a spectral morning suit, Homburg hat and wing-collar, waving a scrap of paper. And he was muttering: "How horrible, fantastic, incredible that we should be digging trenches and filling sandbags here because of a quarrel in a faraway country between people of whom we know nothing." I looked at him – and, indeed, through him. "We are not," I said "we are only considering it." Neville Chamberlain turned, his thin smile even more sepulchral than newsreel memory recalled; hardly surprising, all things considered. "Get a shovel," he said. Whereupon he evaporated, leaving only the scrap of paper fluttering in the air.

I caught it before it hit the ground, and read it through again. Torn out of last Monday's *Times*, it reported that in faraway Cumbria, nudists and ramblers were at war over the latter's right to roam through the former's cherished enclave: the Lakeland Outdoor Club, territory hitherto virgin to big boot, bobble hat, anorak, or indeed anything else, was under threat of invasion by walkers claiming right of way. Now, both sides being people of whom I know nothing – if I have to ramble, it is only as far as the car, and I do it clothed – I shouldn't have given the story a second thought had it not been for its disturbing opening line: "Nudists in the Lake District are celebrating victory." Disturbing not merely for the unsettling speculation as to how nudists do this – lacking hats to chuck in the air, do they hug, jump up and down, spray chilled Bollinger over one another, turn cartwheels? – but for the fact that they have triumphed. A public inquiry by planning inspector Tom Millington (did you have a nice day's inspecting, dear, murmurs Mrs Millington, slippering his weary feet and broaching the Typhoo, oh just the usual, he replies, but his eyes are strangely glazed) has ruled that the Lakeland Outdoor Club is inviolate, and that its members will, but only as far as the ramblers are concerned, have to be skirted.

Why, 300 miles to the unembattled south, should this so

bother me? Because life has taught me, just as it finally taught Neville, that great oaks from little acorns grow, and the next thing you know they are falling on people. And what troubles me is that while ramblers have always been as territorially ambitious as nudists have been secludedly meek, things have suddenly changed: having, thanks to Mr Millington, inherited the earth, the nudist worm within it has turned; it is celebrating victory. This is naturism red in tooth and claw; the sleeping giant of Cerne Abbas has awoken and, along with everything else these days, is going downhill.

And I doubt that we have to look far to understand why naturists – who, just a few short years ago, when *Health & Efficiency* was the only top-shelf magazine, could be observed pursuing a gentle life of meticulous shaving and al fresco ping-pong – have become militant. They have done it because everyone else has. They are fighting for nudist rights. They are insisting that Britain is a multi-apparelled society. I have little doubt that, before very long, we shall see Mr and Mrs Blair, empathetically attired as they always are, visiting a major naturist estate and laughingly tossing a beachball about with community leaders before carefully leaning over the barbecue to select a medium-rare veggieburger and a few spit-roasted sprouts. There will then be a moving speech about inclusiveness and initiatives, and before the month is out not only will nudism be a core subject in the national curriculum, the Armed Forces be required to encourage nude servicemen – with the sensible proviso that they do not volunteer for Trooping the Colour – tuppence be slapped on to tax to deal with NHS waiting-lists inevitably lengthened in winter time, but also, after

170

an inquiry has established that the Met is riddled with institutional dressism, indecent exposure be struck from the statute book.

None of this, mind, will happen until the war is won. The Battle of Lakeland Outdoor Club is not the end, it is not even the beginning of the end, and I rather doubt that it is even the end of the beginning, because ramblers do not take things lying down. They march. That is why I was worrying on the step just now: across the little green octagon is a right of way, and barely a dozen metres from it is a public park, where people often take their clothes off. Ominous, or what? True, I am neutral, but then so was Czechoslovakia. I shall get my shovel. I don't want to be caught with my trousers down.

Last Gasp

THIS may well be the last column I shall ever write. Or not write, because I may well not get to the end of it; and if I do not get to the end of it, it will not appear in tomorrow's paper. If, however, you are now reading it in what tomorrow's paper has become, I will have got to the end of it, because it is, clearly, appearing. At the moment, mind, I have not got to the end of it, so, if you will excuse me, I shall just take a deep breath, slowly, through my nose, hold that breath for a count of three, blow the breath out through my mouth, and repeat this until the tension has disappeared.

Done that. The tension has not disappeared, so if you will just hang on for another tick or two, I shall have a banana.

Done that, now. Feel a lot less tense. I should, of course, have preferred to smoke the banana, but I do not have my banana lighter with me; I always had it with me, up here in my attic sweatshop, in the days when it was a cigarette lighter, and I used it to light the 20 or so – all right, 30 or so – cigarettes I needed to help me write a column: but I gave up smoking five days ago, after 45 years and 400,000 or so – all right 600,000 or so – cigarettes, the purchase price of a new Porsche – all right, a new Ferrari – and now I am on deep breaths and bananas; but I do not know whether deep breaths and bananas will get me to the end of the first article I have ever written, or not written, without cigarettes. I may need plums. Possibly a melon. Plus a brisk walk round the block.

These are all things written on one side of the little card I was given by my doctor when I told him I wanted to give up. The side is headed "Four things to do instead of reaching for a cigarette". I have told you about three of them but I shall not tell you about the fourth thing until I get to the end of this column, so if I do not get to the end of this column you will never know, but if you are reading this, then you will know any minute. Any your minute, that is: I shall not be writing the end of this column until lots of my minutes have passed, because now I am going for a brisk walk round the block.

Done that. Realised, incidentally, that I do not have a block. How big is a block? Have I walked far enough? I shall eat another piece of fruit now, the second thing on the card, but I shall not do the first thing on the card, which is the deep breath thing, because I have just done the third thing on the card, and briskly walking round the block I do not have has left me too knackered to take a deep breath, so I am taking lots of little shallow breaths, hoping this will not bring on a seizure, because it is not easy stuffing a plum down between little shallow breaths. I think I shall stop writing for a bit and turn my card over, because the other side of the card is headed "Emergency reminders procedure", and I do believe this might be an emergency. Under that heading, it says: "I am giving up smoking to (a) improve my health, (b) save money, (c) benefit my family, (d) put me back in control."

That is the sum total of medical advice for the aspirant non-smoker. So if you want to know whether or not the health service is up the spout, you need look no further. I suppose I should count myself lucky my GP didn't put me on a waiting-list for the little card. Hang on a sec, I'm having a grape. Right, where was I? Oh yes, back in control. Well, it's certainly different from the old days when I wasn't in control, I'll say that: I wasn't going nuts, then. Hang on again, sorry, don't go away, I'll be back in a bit.

Hallo again, I have just walked round the block I have not got, eating a Granny Smith and breathing through my nose. It would be hard to describe just how good I feel, now: it must be benefiting my family no end. Perhaps you would care to know that while I walked, I was thinking about the money I will save. I was thinking: it may not be enough for a new Porsche or Ferrari, because I will not live long enough for that, even though I have given up smoking, since the best option is, what, 20 years, always provided I do not drop dead from some fruit-related disease – but in that time I shall probably be able to save enough for a new Vauxhall. So, is looking forward to getting a new Vauxhall at the age of 82 enough of an incentive? Hard to say, but I shall try to stick to my guns, and – oh look, I have got nearly to the end. All that remains is to apologise for using you: for, now that you have also got to the end, I can divulge the fourth thing on the little card, which I promised you all those plums and breaths ago: "Tell as many people as possible," the little card advises, "that you are giving up: knowing they are wondering how long you can last will help you to keep going."

Done that.